D DES

CHRIS ABEL

SKY HIGH: VERTICAL ARCHITECTURE

ROYAL ACADEMY
OF ARTS

1,600m

1,500m

1,400m

1,300m

1,200m

1,100m

1,000m

900m

800m

700m

600m

500m

400m

300m

200m

100m

Monadnock Building, Chicago, 1891
Burnham & Root
66m

Hong Kong and Shaghai Bank,
Hong Kong, 1935
Palmer & Turner
70m

Flatiron Building, New York, 1902
Burnham & Root
93m

Centre Point, London, 1963
Richard Seifert
126m

Pirelli Tower, Milan, 1956
Gio Ponti
127m

Standard Bank, Johannesburg, 1970
Hentrich-Petschnigg & Partners
139m

Chicago Tribune Building, Chicago, 1925
Howells and Hood
141m

Uptown Munchen, Munich, 2003
Ingenhoven Overdiek and Partner
146m

Seagram Building, New York, 1958
Mies van der Rohe and Philip Johnson
158m

Umeda Sky Building, Osaka, 1993
Hiroshi Hara
173m

Marina City, Chicago, 1962
Bertram Goldberg
179m

Hongkong and Shanghai Bank,
Hong Kong, 1986
Foster and Partners
179m

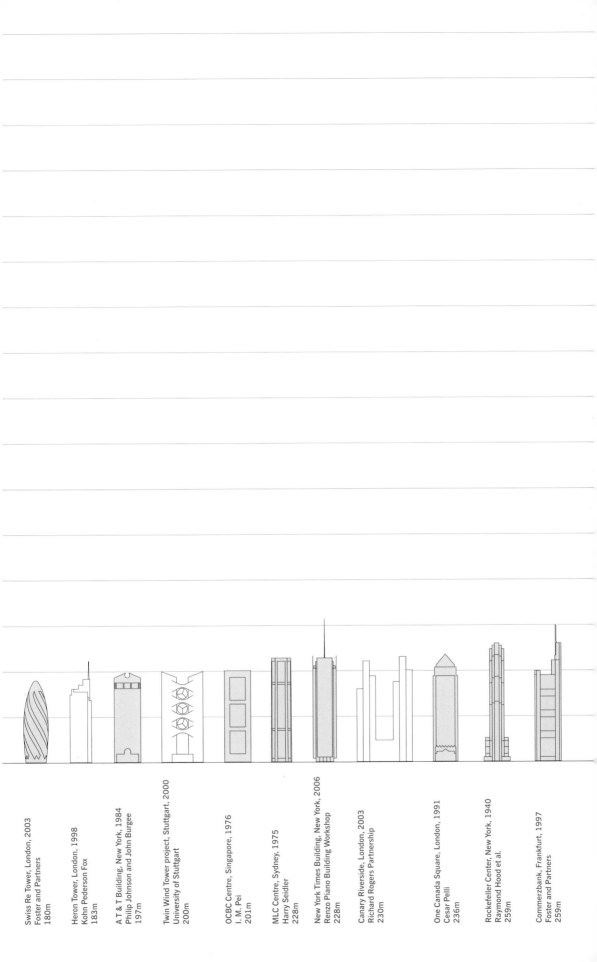

Swiss Re Tower, London, 2003
Foster and Partners
180m

Heron Tower, London, 1998
Kohn Pederson Fox
183m

A T & T Building, New York, 1984
Philip Johnson and John Burgee
197m

Twin Wind Tower project, Stuttgart, 2000
University of Stuttgart
200m

OCBC Centre, Singapore, 1976
I. M. Pei
201m

MLC Centre, Sydney, 1975
Harry Seidler
228m

New York Times Building, New York, 2006
Renzo Piano Building Workshop
228m

Canary Riverside, London, 2003
Richard Rogers Partnership
230m

One Canada Square, London, 1991
Cesar Pelli
236m

Rockefeller Center, New York, 1940
Raymond Hood et al.
259m

Commerzbank, Frankfurt, 1997
Foster and Partners
259m

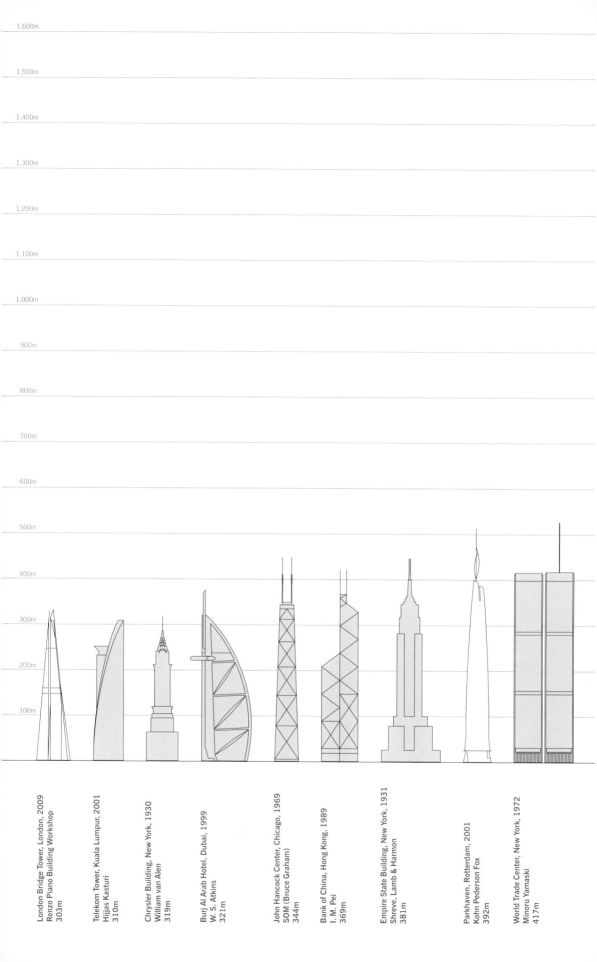

1,600m

1,500m

1,400m

1,300m

1,200m

1,100m

1,000m

900m

800m

700m

600m

500m

400m

300m

200m

100m

London Bridge Tower, London, 2009
Renzo Piano Building Workshop
303m

Telekom Tower, Kuala Lumpur, 2001
Hijjas Kasturi
310m

Chrysler Building, New York, 1930
William van Alen
319m

Burj Al Arab Hotel, Dubai, 1999
W. S. Atkins
321m

John Hancock Center, Chicago, 1969
SOM (Bruce Graham)
344m

Bank of China, Hong Kong, 1989
I. M. Pei
369m

Empire State Building, New York, 1931
Shreve, Lamb & Harmon
381m

Parkhaven, Rotterdam, 2001
Kohn Pederson Fox
392m

World Trade Center, New York, 1972
Minoru Yamaski
417m

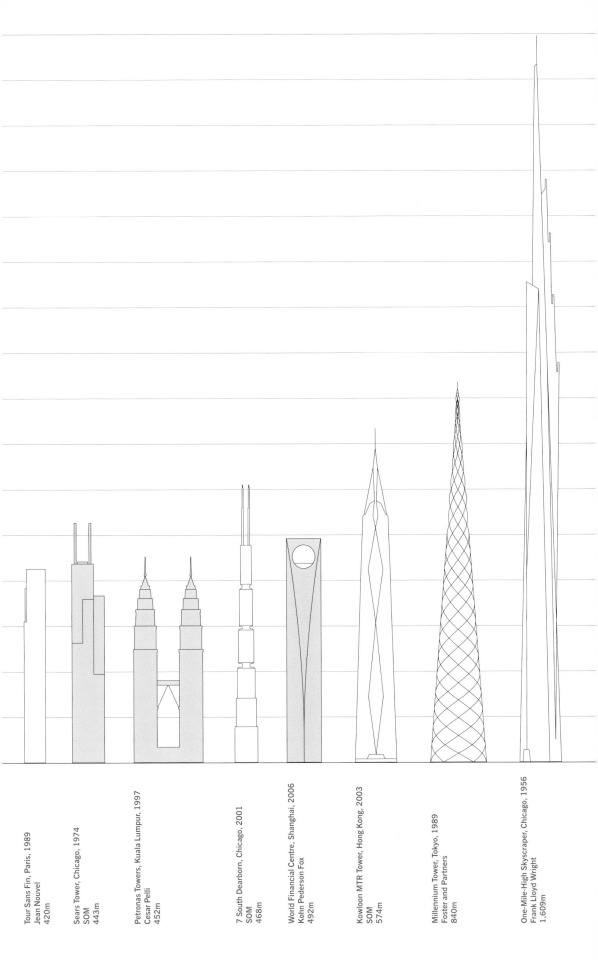

Tour Sans Fin, Paris, 1989
Jean Nouvel
420m

Sears Tower, Chicago, 1974
SOM
443m

Petronas Towers, Kuala Lumpur, 1997
Cesar Pelli
452m

7 South Dearborn, Chicago, 2001
SOM
468m

World Financial Centre, Shanghai, 2006
Kohn Pederson Fox
492m

Kowloon MTR Tower, Hong Kong, 2003
SOM
574m

Millennium Tower, Tokyo, 1989
Foster and Partners
840m

One-Mile-High Skyscraper, Chicago, 1956
Frank Lloyd Wright
1,609m

First published on the occasion
of the exhibition *Sky High*
Royal Academy of Arts, London
2 June – 10 August 2003

Exhibition Curators
Norman Foster
with Chris Abel
MaryAnne Stevens

Exhibition Organisers
Katy Harris
Sally Kennedy

**Picture Research, Photographic and
Copyright Coordination**
Matthew Foreman

Catalogue
Royal Academy Publications
Harry Burden
Carola Krueger
Fiona McHardy
Peter Sawbridge
Nick Tite

Copy-editing and Proofreading
Philippa Baker

Book Design
Esterson Lackersteen

Colour Origination
DawkinsColour

Printed in Italy by Graphicom
All texts by Chris Abel: © Chris Abel
and Royal Academy of Arts, 2003

Line drawings on pages 2–5 by
John Hewitt

Editorial Note
The date given for each of the projects
represents the completion date.

British Library Cataloguing-in-
Publication Data

A catalogue record for this book is available
from the British Library

ISBN 1-903973-33-3

Distributed outside the
United States and Canada by
Thames & Hudson Ltd, London
Distributed in the
United States and Canada by
Harry N. Abrams, Inc., New York

Acknowledgements
The Royal Academy of Arts would like to
acknowledge with thanks the advice and
support of the Architecture Committee of
the Royal Academy of Arts, Prof Alexander
Cuthbert, Alan Davidson, Paul Finch, Ada
Fung, David Jenkins, Liu Thai Ker, Chris
McCarthy, Jeremy Melvin, Peter Murray,
Tom Phillips RA, Norman Rosenthal,
Deyan Sudjic, the Venice Biennale and
John Zukowsky.

Lenders
Allies and Morrison, Anthony Ng Architects,
Architectures Jean Nouvel, Bank of China,
Broadway Malyan, Cesar Pelli & Associates,
Charles Correa Associates, Commerzbank,
Dominique Perrault Architecte, Foster and
Partners, Grimshaw, Hentrich-Petschnigg
& Partners, Hijjas Kasturi Associates,
Ingenhoven Overdiek and Partner, Jumeirah
International, Kohn Pedersen Fox Associates,
Mori Building Co., M3 Architects, Marks
Barfield Architects, Massimiliano Fuksas
Architteto, Mecanoo Architects, Powerhouse
Museum, Rafael Viñoly Architects, Renzo
Piano Building Workshop, Richard Rogers
Partnership, Skidmore, Owings, & Merrill,
T. R. Hamzah & Yeang, University of
Stuttgart, United Architects, Wilkinson
Eyre Architects Ltd.

The Royal Academy of Arts is also grateful
to the following for their generous support
of the exhibition:

Supporters
The Drue Heinz Endowment for Architecture
The Sherling Charitable Trust

CONTENTS

FOREWORD

The urge to build tall is not new. It is inherent within us – part of the same drive that leads us to climb mountains or to explore outer space. It starts as children with building blocks or sandcastles as we attempt to push materials further and further. This is echoed in the technology of historical structures. From Stonehenge and the Pyramids to the great medieval cathedrals, stone was extended as far as it could go. Load-bearing brick was pushed to its limits – a height of sixteen storeys – in the Monadnock Building in Chicago. Wrought iron was taken to a height of 325 metres in the Eiffel Tower. Steel was stretched to its limits in the Sears Tower and a composite of steel and concrete supports the Petronas Towers – currently the world's tallest buildings. In one sense there is a delight in making technology and materials work as hard as possible simply because we can – something that dates back to the so-called ages of pre-civilisation and has been unstoppable ever since.

However, at the beginning of the twenty-first century there are far more urgent reasons for building tall: cultural, demographic, environmental and economic. Two vital factors are global population growth and the increasing rate of urbanisation. The world's population has doubled to 6 billion since 1960 and is currently growing at the rate of 78 million a year – a pattern that is expected to continue for at least the next decade. Hand in hand with this trend is a worldwide shift towards living in cities. It is estimated that by 2030 two thirds of the world's population will be urbanised. While established giants such as London continue to expand, we are already beginning to see the growth of a new generation of megacities of unprecedented size, and urban conurbations in excess of 25 million people are predicted in the next fifteen years. The major challenge in such cities is to accommodate more and more people at greater densities than before while seeking to create a higher quality of urban life. While the tall building may not be the only key, with finite resources and with less and less land on which to build it is a vital component of the future city.

Energy consumption and atmospheric pollution are also key issues. In the developed world buildings account for half the energy we consume. The remainder is divided between transport and industry and these factors are linked in a complex chain. As cities spread horizontally and their populations spend more time in their cars travelling to and from work, levels of energy consumption – in the form of fossil fuels – and pollution rise inexorably. By building to greater densities and to higher levels of energy efficiency in urban centres that have established public transport systems we can reduce reliance on the car with all its attendant problems. We can also improve the quality of urban life, bringing down travel times and allowing people to live, work and spend their leisure time in close proximity.

It is interesting to note the shifting geographical spread of tall buildings in the last two decades and the changing attitudes to skyscrapers around the world. The long-established centres in the West – New York and Chicago – have fast been overtaken by the rush to build tall in Asia and the Pacific Rim. China alone has 22 of the world's hundred tallest buildings, second only to America, and cities such as Shanghai have been transformed beyond recognition. In ten years Pudong, Shanghai's new business district which now bristles with a forest of tall buildings, has gained the kind of skyline that took 50 years to achieve in New York and 30 years in Hong Kong.

While few people would welcome the arrival of the skyscraper in sensitive city centres such as Florence or Istanbul, the last few years have witnessed a radical change in attitudes to tall buildings in some of Europe's oldest cities. Madrid and Barcelona, for example, have announced plans for a series of towers to meet their shortage of flexible modern office space.

London, long resistant to upward growth, has recently approved the construction of a wave of tall buildings.

Among the most recent proposals is Renzo Piano's London Bridge Tower. If built, this 66-storey building will provide living and working accommodation for 8,000 people. It will be sited above an existing transport hub – one of the busiest train, Underground and bus stations in the capital – and will have no car parking. Instead, its occupants will use the city's public transport arteries, thus avoiding additional congestion and pollution. The low-rise, low-density alternative would be to accommodate all those people in conventional developments outside the city centre in the suburbs or the green belt, consuming twenty times the amount of land.

This exhibition and book come at a crucial moment in the development of our cities. Together they present an argument in favour of higher densities and taller structures, not because such approaches are the ultimate expression of the Modernist project or of a particular aesthetic, but because they can help to solve the problem of growth in our cities. That is not to understate the role that aesthetics has to play – tall buildings have a far greater visual impact on our cities than any other structure. It is for this reason that we have compiled an international survey of historical and recent examples – many of them icons of their respective cities – that have shaped the development of this vitally important building type.

1
INTRODUCTION

Supreme achievements of engineering and design, corporate icons, expressions of modernity and civic pride, real-estate bonanzas, familiar and reassuring landmarks, potent symbols, testimonies to the human spirit – whether any or all of these things, skyscrapers arouse more controversy than any other building form.

Love them or hate them, one thing we cannot do is ignore them. And they suddenly seem to be getting a lot bigger and more numerous. After a century in which Chicago and New York remained unchallenged as home to the world's tallest and best-known modern towers, many cities around the globe are fiercely competing for the title – nowhere more so than in Asia Pacific, where the crown has already been snatched from America by Kuala Lumpur's twin Petronas Towers (1, 2), with Shanghai next in line.

If this contest were simply a matter of size and ego, the criticism often aimed at skyscrapers would be well deserved. Yet the race for the clouds obscures the more profound changes taking place in the design and construction of tall buildings involving the creation of whole new genres, and the important issues underlying those changes. Where all large towers were once designed and built more or less the same way, with standard plans and parts, many of the structures built during recent years differ radically both from each other and from anything that went before them. Some are not shaped like towers at all and, like the new genres of skyscraper, are better described more broadly as vertical architecture. Where once they were built solely to provide more downtown office space, many now house numerous different activities, including public functions and spaces, and may not even be sited in urban areas.

Significantly, where skyscrapers once consumed enormous amounts of the fossil fuels that produce greenhouse gases, they are now increasingly designed to minimise energy consumption and will in future also generate a growing share of their own power from renewable sources. Many architects and urbanists now regard tall buildings not so much as forms created in opposition to nature, as they were once perceived, but as essential elements in a sustainable or ecologically friendly strategy for urban design. In particular, they are seen as an important part of the solution to out-of-control urban growth in both the developed and developing world, where the combination of vast megacities with populations numbering tens of millions and a chronic shortage of open land is critical.

This book, written for the Royal Academy of Arts' show of the same title as part of the *Summer Exhibition 2003*, traces the evolution of vertical architecture around the world, from the first iconic skyscrapers in Chicago and New York to the present day, and examines what this process tells us about our changing values and cities. These developments are explained not through abstract arguments and statistics (mostly restricted here to the discussion of megacities, where they are unavoidable), but through key exemplars, both familiar and not so familiar, which present clear evidence of those changes.

The selection of examples is as wide ranging as the nature and diversity of the building form calls for, covering many parts of the world and many quite different design approaches representing conflicting values as well as different periods in time. While the book does not purport to include every tall building or related development of significance – that would take a much larger book – it is hoped that, like the exhibition, it will help to focus minds and stimulate debate about this fast-changing architectural form.

2
ORIGINS AND DIVERSIFICATION

4
Equitable Building,
1915, New York,
by Ernest Graham.
The sheer building
overshadowed its
neighbours and led
to the introduction
of setbacks

3
Previous page:
'Flatiron' Building,
1902, New York,
by Daniel Burnham

The new genres of vertical architecture have their origins in a chain of broader urban developments going back well over a hundred years. It is a popular myth, often shared by designers themselves, that skyscrapers were conceived by architects obsessed with building higher than before, and that most tall buildings in the world are the product of their professional culture and ambitions, together with those of the engineers with whom they work.

Appealing as such myths are, the real picture is both more complex and a great deal more challenging. Skyscrapers are no more the sole product of architects' or engineers' imaginations than are any other familiar building type, such as dwellings, schools, factories, railway stations and airports. Rather, they are the outcome of a combination of historical, social, economic and technological factors – over most of which professional designers have no direct control – which taken together amount to a modern vernacular. Given sufficient determination and talent, architects can influence the design of tall buildings in substantial ways to help create a better environment, creating iconic works in the process. Ultimately, however, it is the larger course of events in the world that have shaped the nature and form of vertical architecture, just as they shape our wider environment.

Key inventions
The first tall buildings in late nineteenth-century Chicago arose from the simple fact that, as in cities all over the world, people willingly congregated there in large numbers to seek work, do business and enjoy the diverse social and cultural attractions that only cities can offer. Development was spurred by the emergence during the same period of large industrial and financial organisations requiring headquarters and office buildings located in city centres close to related organisations. Situated strategically in

the centre of the North American continent on the main transcontinental railway and water routes connecting with the productive hinterlands of Canada and the other American states, Chicago was one of the fastest growing cities in the world by the beginning of the twentieth century. As the city grew, so did its buildings. Inevitably, more people wanted to occupy the same choice pieces of land than could be accommodated by smaller buildings, so they built higher and higher, or at least as high as economics and current technologies allowed.

The most important factors in skyscraper development during these early years were the invention of the iron frame, which displaced solid, load-bearing walls, and above all the Otis mechanical lift (7) – both engineers' and industrialists' creations – followed by the widespread use of rolled steel and reinforced concrete. They were supplemented by the

5
New York Life Building, 1895, New York, by William Le Baron Jenney, an early example of stone cladding over a steel frame, called 'curtain walling'

'curtain wall' (5), which was hung from the exterior frame at each floor. Having no structural purpose, it could be made of thinly cut stone, glass and metal or any other material, mass-produced or otherwise as needed, allowing designers free rein to do as they pleased with the façade. All three inventions and the tall buildings they made possible were in turn the outcome of America's growing economic and industrial strength, which were to make it the leading world power of the twentieth century.

Architects at this time played a relatively minor role in the evolution of skyscraper design, and were mostly concerned with cloaking the unruly newcomers with a socially acceptable dress – usually modified versions of the architectural languages with which they were already familiar. Daniel Burnham's 'Flatiron' Building (3, 6) of 1902, named after the pointed shape induced by its triangular site, was one of New York's first tall buildings to have an all-steel frame but is equally famed for the tripartite vertical division of its stone cladding. Structured in the manner of a classical Greek column into three parts – bottom (base), middle (shaft) and top (entablature) – the division happily expressed the different conditions at each level: street and entrances, repetitive floors and crowning glory.

Two neo-Gothic extravaganzas – the Woolworth Building of 1913 in New York, by Cass Gilbert, and the Chicago Tribune Tower (8), of 1925 in Chicago, by Raymond Hood and John Mead Howells – gave rise to the apt description, 'cathedrals of commerce'. But it was New York's unneighbourly Equitable Building (4) of 1915, by Ernest Graham, with its extreme plot ratio and overshadowing sheer walls, that ultimately shaped the future of skyscraper design for much of the century. Designed to provide the maximum possible amount of rentable space on a given plot, its only saving grace was the public arcade that cut right through it at ground level.

6
'Flatiron' Building, 1902, New York, by Daniel Burnham. The building takes its shape and nickname from its triangular site

7
Otis mechanical lift, 1854. Elisha Graves Otis's invention of the safe lift removed any human limitations on building height

9
Chrysler Building,
1930, New York,
by William van
Alen, a definitive
Art Deco design

8
Chicago Tribune
Tower, 1925,
Chicago, by
Raymond Hood
and John Mead
Howells, one of
several neo-Gothic
designs dubbed
'cathedrals of
commerce'

The indifference shown by the Equitable's owners to the effect of their building on its surroundings was too much to swallow, even for *laissez-faire* New York. Thereafter, all tall buildings in the city over a certain height had to be set back in stages to allow sufficient daylight to reach the streets and adjacent buildings – guidelines quickly adopted by other cities. As a consequence, aside from their much-admired pinnacles and other Art Deco features, the Chrysler Building (9) of 1930, by William van Alen, and the Empire State Building (10, 11) of 1931, by Shreve, Lamb & Harmon, owe their distinctive narrowing profiles as much to New York's building laws of the time as to any other consideration.

Breaking the mould

Despite differences in height and external appearance, all these early towers share the same kebab-like structural arrangement developed in Chicago, with stacks of identical floors of decreasing area supported by evenly spaced columns and a central core containing lifts, stairways and vertical services. Eventually, more adventurous architects were to challenge the standard model for tall buildings, launching a process of intermittent reinvention of the type that continues to this day. Sometimes motivated to apply an architectural approach refined on other building types, or driven to experiment with new technologies and forms in order to reach higher than before, or compelled to

[handwritten note:] Points came through Planning laws for light not do do with centres of gravity.

10
Empire State
Building, 1931,
New York, by
Shreve, Lamb &
Harmon, an iconic
skyscraper and
the world's tallest
building for
nearly 40 years

12
Rockefeller Center,
1940, New York,
by Raymond Hood
and associates.
The pedestrianised
complex includes
a square that
converts to a
skating rink
in winter

11
Previous page:
Empire State
Building, 1931,
New York, by
Shreve, Lamb
& Harmon

13
Glass skyscraper
project, 1921,
Berlin, by Mies
van der Rohe for
the Friedrichstrasse
skyscraper
competition.
The first glass-
walled tower, it was
not realised for over
30 years

14
Larkin Building,
1903, Buffalo,
by Frank Lloyd
Wright. It was
another 80 years
before these
spatial principles
were applied to
skyscrapers

15
Plain Voisin,
1925, Paris, by
Le Corbusier. The
cruciform towers
anticipate Hong
Kong's later
mass housing
programme

16
Lake Shore Drive
Apartments, 1951,
Chicago, by Mies
van der Rohe.
Mies's first
American buildings
are a far cry from
his free-form
Berlin project

rethink their approach by changing social or cultural circumstances, innovative designers frequently broke the mould. In the process, they created new forms that would in turn become the standard and model for others to follow or to try to improve, producing a new genre and a whole series of related designs.

While it does not qualify by height, Frank Lloyd Wright's Larkin Building (14) of 1903 in Buffalo, with its full-height atrium, open office floors and peripheral service towers, was an important precedent for future office towers, changing the relationship between space, structure and services. Where people working in conventional office buildings were separated from each other at every floor level, Wright adapted the flowing spatial concepts of his 'organic' architecture to the office, creating a unitary central space that bound everyone in the building visibly together – an arrangement as pleasing to unions as to managers.

Though each of its component structures has a conventional format, the Rockefeller Center (12) of 1940 in New York, by Raymond Hood et al., created a different kind of model: an enlightened exercise in urban design involving the first fully integrated cluster of tall buildings rather than a single tower. With its public open space (which converts to a skating rink in winter), extensive, multilevel pedestrian links and numerous shops, cafés and restaurants, it was the first skyscraper project to give as much to the public as to the private realm.

In Europe, the two glass skyscraper projects of 1921 (13) and 1922 for Berlin, by Mies van der Rohe, and the rows of cruciform skyscrapers in Le Corbusier's Plain Voisin (15) of 1925, together with the latter's tower project for Algiers of 1939, forecasted the shape of things to come. In their unusual plan forms and in their reflective, all-glass curtain walls, Mies's skyscrapers, while inspired by Chicago's skyline, were quite unlike

anything yet built there. But Mies's vision was not to be realised in the same form. By the time he came to build his Lake Shore Drive Apartments (16) in 1951 in Chicago he had traded in his dynamic compositions for a Modernised neoclassicism and a relatively ordinary structural plan, preferring the refinements of steel and glass detail to more radical approaches.

Post-war decades
It was left to Gordon Bunshaft of Skidmore, Owings, & Merrill (SOM) to give the curtain-walled glass skyscraper its definitive post-war Modernist form in the Lever House (17) of 1952 in New York. Comprising a narrow, tall slab rising through a single-storey raised podium with an open, semi-private courtyard in the centre, the dynamic composition embodied the forward-looking and civic-minded spirit of early Modernism and related equally to street and sky. It was followed by Mies's more stately Seagram Building (18) of 1958, also in New York, with its generous open plaza – a clear if delayed riposte to the Equitable's egocentric design. Together with the Rockefeller Center, these tall buildings proved that private ambition was not always incompatible with the public good.

As well as spawning such defining works, the post-war decades were among the most innovative periods in vertical architecture, yielding a host of experimental designs and new genres. First came Wright's project of 1956 for a One-Mile-High Skyscraper (20) for the outskirts of Chicago – a dramatic counterpoint to his low-density Utopian project, Broadacre City. Supported by a reinforced-concrete tapered structure shaped like a tripod, the slender tower is the precursor of more recent megatowers. To solve the problem of moving up and down such enormous distances, he conceived atomic-powered lifts running on vertical tracks carrying

17
Lever House,
1952, New York,
by Skidmore,
Owings, & Merrill.
The completely
sealed, glass-and-
metal, curtain-
walled skyscraper
was designed to
be fully air-
conditioned

18
Seagram Building,
1958, New York,
by Mies van der
Rohe with Philip
Johnson. The
curtain-walled
façade has
protruding
I-beams, creating
an illusion of
solidity when
viewed on angle

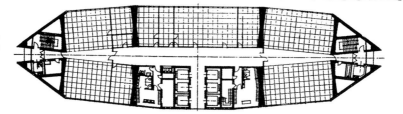

19
Price Tower, 1956, Bartlesville, by Frank Lloyd Wright. This stand-alone tower showed that apartment towers need not necessarily be built in cities

20
One-Mile-High Skyscraper project, 1956, Chicago, by Frank Lloyd Wright, the model for recent megatowers and 'vertical cities'

21
Pirelli Tower, 1956, Milan, by Gio Ponti. The tapered structure expresses the decreasing loads towards the top

22
Tomorrow's City Hall project, 1952, Philadelphia, by Louis Kahn. The eccentric structure prefigures contemporary experimental designs

23
Center City
Philadelphia
project, 1952,
Philadelphia,
by Louis Kahn,
an attempt to
accommodate
private
automobiles
in cities through
vertical parking

a hundred passengers each. Unjustified by pressures on either land or fuel, both then plentiful and cheap, the hugely ambitious project is the exception to the rule: more the fruit of Wright's own restless and contradictory imagination than the product of any of American society's more urgent needs, though it might now be appreciated as ahead of its time.

At the other end of the scale, Wright's Price Tower (19) of 1956 in Oklahoma shared with his earlier residential St Mark's Tower an unusual design based on four radiating structural fins and mezzanine floor plans, but mixed several floors of offices for its corporate owners with the apartments. Standing alone in the small town of Bartlesville, Wright's articulated, tree-like structure suggested – like the One-Mile-High project – a wholly new and prescient conception of the role and placement of tall buildings, both as an alternative to the low-rise suburb and as a practical way of providing living space and preserving open land in the same stroke.

Louis Kahn's Center City Philadelphia project (23) of 1952 is a bold but ultimately doomed attempt to deal with the American preference for private automobiles over public transportation, incorporating vertical parking in great drum-like, mixed-use, tall structures. The scheme included Kahn's Tomorrow's City Hall project (22), which was, besides Wright's One-Mile-High tower, the boldest exercise in vertical architecture proposed until then. Supported by a zigzagging, triangulated steel structure, the strikingly eccentric form prefigures contemporary cutting-edge designs.

The 1950s and early 1960s also saw Europeans taking their first hesitant steps in the field, with four notable reinforced-concrete designs by different architects, each setting its own distinctive precedent. The best known of these, the elegant Pirelli Tower (21) of 1956 in Milan, by Gio Ponti with engineer Pier Luigi Nervi,

is a slim, sharp-ended slab supported by two sets of tapering cross walls. The first of a series of towers – most of which were subsequently built in Australia – engineered by Nervi to express the changing vertical loads on the structure, the Pirelli Tower provided column-free, full-width spaces that allowed natural light to penetrate into its centre, greatly improving the quality of the working environment, as well as offering views through both sides.

The Thyssenhaus (24) of 1957 in Düsseldorf, by Hentrich-Petschnigg & Partners, was designed to look like three closely packed, parallel narrow slabs but in fact has an integrated open plan, allowing ample daylight to penetrate the interior as well as views right through – much like the

24
Thyssenhaus,
1957, Düsseldorf,
by Hentrich-
Petschnigg &
Partners. The
appearance of
three thin slabs
disguises a single,
open, well-lit plan

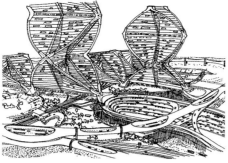

Pirelli Tower. Like the contemporary and more familiar United Nations Headquarters of 1953 in New York, by Harrison and Abramovitz with Le Corbusier and others, the Thyssenhaus stands by itself overlooking open spaces and was clearly influenced by the former's crisp design with its thin, solid end walls.

Designed to complement historical as well as modern buildings on the Milan skyline, the neo-Gothic Torre Velasca (26) of 1958, by BBPR Architects, has an exposed frame with an enlarged upper section supported by angled struts. One of a kind, the articulated tower, with its vaguely medieval appearance and pitched roof complete with 'chimneys', anticipated the historicism of later movements but has a structural integrity usually lacking in projects of that ilk.

Lastly, the much-maligned Centre Point (27) of 1963 in London, by Richard Seifert, suffered from being left empty for too long after it was completed – a financial ploy on the part of its owners – its reputation further tainted by its windswept underpass and base, the result of uncontrolled down draughts. Recently refurbished, it is enjoying renewed appreciation as London's first serious tall building.

If the innovative vertical architecture of these years was mostly marked by exceptional individual structures, the avant-garde designs of the 1960s were dominated by megastructures – collections of towers and other tall buildings all integrated into a shared three-dimensional infrastructure. While Kahn's Philadelphia project is sometimes considered to belong in this category, the megastructure concept had its strongest supporters elsewhere. In Europe, partly inspired by the Futurist architectural schemes of Antonio Sant'Elia, the British Archigram group produced numerous imaginative schemes, of which their City Interchange project (28) of 1963, with its

joined-up towers grouped around a transportation node, has proved to be the most accurate in anticipating future developments.

In Japan the Metabolists, a disparate group of individual architects named after the biological models of growth and change that inspired their work, created similar complex urban structures, though with a clear preference for reinforced concrete over the lightweight steel structures favoured by Archigram. The vast Tokyo Bay project of 1960, by Kenzo Tange, and the twisting towers of the Helix City project (25) of 1961 for the Ginza district of Tokyo, by Kisho Kurokawa, are just two of the movement's iconic works. Though none of Archigram's schemes and few of the Metabolists' were ever realised, and even then only in disappointing fragments, both groups exerted a strong influence on later developments.

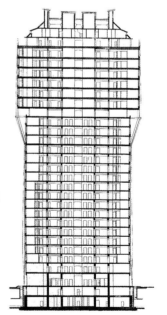

26
Torre Velasca,
1958, Milan, by
BBPR Architects.
The neo-Gothic
design heralded
future historicist
approaches

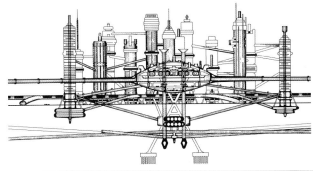

28
City Interchange
project, 1963,
by Archigram, a
visionary project
anticipating
current schemes
based on major
interchanges

27
Centre Point,
1963, London,
by Richard Seifert.
London's first
skyscraper was
derided for years
as a windswept,
empty building

Second golden age

During the same period American designers also produced a number of canonical buildings – the most important owing as much, if not more, to the engineers involved as to their architects – reaffirming America's position as world leader in vertical architecture.

The twin towers of Marina City (29) of 1962 in Chicago, by Bertram Goldberg with engineers Severud et al., are significant both for being among the first high-density residential buildings built in an American city centre and for their circular, reinforced-concrete structures. Part of a large mixed-use development, the two towers stand on a podium providing public access to the harbour front and ferries. The lower part of each tower is used for residents' parking – shades of Kahn's Philadelphia project – while the apartments with their distinctive circular balconies (known locally as 'corn cobs') take up the rest of the building. The large cylindrical cores provide greater resistance against horizontal wind forces – a major problem in tall buildings – than conventional smaller cores, acting like cantilevered hollow beams fixed to the ground. The structural efficiency of the design resulted in considerable savings in construction costs in comparison with a normal structure.

Marina City marked the beginning of the second 'golden age' of Chicago skyscrapers, but it was two steel-framed buildings designed by Bruce Graham of SOM with Fazlur Khan, the celebrated Pakistan-born engineer, that most clearly confirmed the city's pride of place in the skies. Also specially designed to resist wind forces, the John Hancock Center (30, 32) of 1969 is structured like a giant oil rig in which the main loads are transferred to the large corner columns and cross-braces. The handsome tapered shape adds to the structural stability but was principally devised to accommodate the different spatial requirements of its various functions: small spaces for the apartments in the upper levels, large spaces for commercial uses and parking in the lowest levels, and medium-sized spaces for the offices in between.

SOM and Khan's other masterpiece, the 443-metre-high Sears Tower (31) of 1974, which was the tallest building in the world until the Petronas Towers were built, has yet another type of structure that is even more effective against wind forces. Adopting a similar principle to that used in the tubular core of the Marina Centre, the Sears Tower consists of nine steel-framed 'bundled tubes' with square plans or 'sections' (if read as beams cantilevered from the ground, which is how they actually behave), all acting in unison to strengthen greatly the inherent stiffness of the whole. Each tube stops at a different height in a series of great steps until only two joined elements remain, terminating together at the hundredth floor.

The ill-fated twin towers of the World Trade Center (33, 35) of 1972 and 1973, by Minoru Yamasaki with Emery Roth and engineers Skilling Helle, Christiansen and Robertson, were designed according to similar principles. Each tower behaved as a cantilevered steel-framed tube, the densely columned exterior walls effectively acting like a continuous membrane, taking both dead loads and wind loads together. (It was the damage to this vital membrane, combined with the enormous temperatures generated by burning aviation fuel, that caused their collapse.) The World Trade Center towers demonstrated the aesthetic attractions of this kind of structure, achieving a slimmer and more graceful height-to-width ratio than can be achieved with conventional kebab-type structures. Until the tragic events of 11 September 2001, they were an inseparable part of the Manhattan skyline, a symbol of human ingenuity and daring as much as the global culture that gave rise to them.

29
Marina City, 1962, Chicago, by Bertram Goldberg. The twin concrete-framed towers were the first to employ a tube-within-a-tube structure

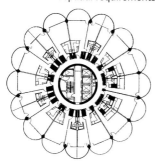

31
Sears Tower,
1974, Chicago,
by Skidmore,
Owings, & Merrill.
The 'bundled tube'
structure gives
it great strength
against wind forces

32
Following page:
John Hancock
Center, 1969,
Chicago, by
Skidmore, Owings
& Merrill

30
John Hancock
Center, 1969,
Chicago, by
Skidmore, Owings,
& Merrill. The
braced structure
resembles a giant
oil rig

33
World Trade
Center, 1972
and 1973, New
York, by Minoru
Yamasaki with
Emery Roth. The
slim twin towers
were an integral
part of the
Manhattan skyline

The Hancock Center, Sears Tower and World
Trade Center marked the literal apex of American
twentieth-century skyscraper design – tangible
expressions of confidence and faith in a future
shaped by American culture and technology.
The A T & T Building (34) (now the Sony
Building) of 1984 in New York, by Philip
Johnson and John Burgee, signalled a different
set of priorities. Partly as a result of poorly built
and aesthetically dull high-rise developments,
the 1960s and 1970s had seen a steady
decline of public and professional confidence
in orthodox Modernism and a revival of interest
in historical architecture. (Yamasaki had already
acknowledged the trend with his neo-Gothic
detailing of the World Trade Center façades.)
The Postmodern backlash, manifested in

buildings like the A T & T, often involved
borrowing past styles or motifs and distorting
them for rhetorical effect. A light-hearted return
to the tripartite façadism of early skyscraper
design, Johnson and Burgee's historicist
approach entrenched a division of labour
that is, if not peculiar to America, then certainly
common practice there, by which architects are
mostly left to dress a building while its other
features and construction are worked out
independently by others.
    Thereafter the initiative in vertical architecture,
in the contest for both sheer height and, more
importantly, innovative design, was to pass
elsewhere, to a different part of the world, though
some Western architects and engineers would
continue to be involved at the cutting edge.

35
Following page:
World Trade
Center, 1972
and 1973, New
York, by Minoru
Yamasaki with
Emery Roth

34
A T & T Building,
1984, New York,
by Philip Johnson
and John Burgee,
an eccentric
return to the
tripartite concept
of external design

37
Hongkong and
Shanghai Bank,
1935, Hong Kong,
by Palmer &
Turner, the tallest
and most advanced
structure outside
the West for
many years

36
Previous page:
Bank of China,
1989, Hong Kong,
by I. M. Pei.
The Hong Kong
Club and Office
Building, 1984,
by Harry Seidler,
is on the left

Just as the first skyscrapers marked the rising economic and cultural power of America, so the next significant phase in the evolution of vertical architecture around the globe symbolised the rising fortunes of the countries of Asia Pacific.

In 1982 BBC Radio broadcast a landmark series called *The People of the Pacific Century*, followed soon after by a television series and book on the same theme. The first of a stream of similar analyses, the two series focused on the region's extraordinary growth and potential future impact on the world. The global centre of economic and cultural energy, they argued, was shifting inexorably from the countries bordering the Atlantic to those bordering the Pacific. The 'Pacific Century', otherwise known as the 'Pacific Age', was born.

Changing skylines
While California and its high-tech economy is also included in this picture, it was Japan and the Asian Pacific countries, most of all the 'Four Tigers' – Hong Kong, Taiwan, South Korea and Singapore – that caught observers' imaginations. Over most of the following two decades, the BBC's analysis proved to be extraordinarily accurate. The 'Four Tigers' were joined in the late 1980s by a resurgent China, now displacing a faltering Japan as the primary engine of growth in the region and well on the way to overtaking America as the world's largest economy.

The rapid pace of development in Asia Pacific could be readily seen in the changing skylines of its major cities, which began to rival New York's and Chicago's, throwing down a highly visible

High-density
housing, 1980s,
Hong Kong,
by Hong Kong
Housing Authority.
Overcrowding
led to a massive
programme of
high-rise housing,
such as these
cruciform towers

gauntlet and putting into question the West's supremacy. After pausing for a while in the aftermath of the 1997 international financial crisis, most of the Asian Pacific countries are once again forging ahead with growth rates Western governments would covet, casting up ever higher buildings in the process as if to make the point.

The upward surge in the region's economy and buildings was portended as long ago as 1935 with the completion of the second headquarters building for the Hongkong and Shanghai Bank (37) in central Hong Kong, by local expatriate firm Palmer & Turner. Compelled to turn skywards by the acute shortage of buildable land on Hong Kong Island, Palmer & Turner built the tallest structure between Cairo and San Francisco at the time. An Art Deco design, it was the first building outside America to use high-tensile steel. It also had high-speed lifts, air-conditioning and other state-of-the-art features seldom found in Asia. The pride of the building, in addition to its technical features, was its great vaulted banking hall, reminiscent of the buildings of ancient Rome.

High-density housing
However, significant though the bank was, the next and more important steps in high-density vertical architecture in Hong Kong were not in the private realm but in the public realm of state-built housing – and on an unprecedented scale. Until the early 1950s, the only decent housing was constructed by private firms for government employees and the more affluent business classes, usually in multistorey blocks and towers, many of which were clustered around Hong Kong Island's famous Peak, overlooking and within easy reach of the central city. The vast majority of the working population lived, as most poor people still do in the developing world, as squatters on 'empty' land in surrounding areas,

in flimsy shacks, without clean water supplies, drainage or other basic amenities.

Floods of new immigrants into Hong Kong from communist China after the Second World War aggravated the problem. In December 1953 a terrible fire in one of the colony's largest squatter settlements on the mainland in Kowloon left 53,000 people homeless, finally forcing the government into action. A state-subsidised programme to resettle squatters was quickly undertaken, beginning with 'walk-up', six- and seven-storey, concrete-framed, H-shaped blocks, dubbed the 'Mark I' type. Providing a minimal 2.23 square metres per adult in single-room units on double-loaded corridors, the simple, inexpensive blocks offered electric lighting, clean water on tap and hygienic toilets and washrooms, the latter facilities being placed in shared blocks at the end of each corridor.

Beginning with these humble but effective measures, the newly formed Hong Kong Housing Authority and the Public Works Department together initiated a major programme of urban renewal and low-cost housing for both public and private ownership. In little more than a decade they transformed Hong Kong from a medium-rise city of four to five storeys to a high-density city of over twenty storeys, with buildings often housing shops, offices and schools as well as living quarters within the same structure. As the colony prospered, so the housing programme was upgraded. Slim tower blocks with lifts (38) and more spacious units took the place of the early basic types, and a series of improved housing standards and new types was developed, mostly designed, following UK practice, by the Housing Authority's own architects.

Singular achievements
While the public housing authorities in Hong Kong were changing the entire built landscape of the small colony, individual projects, in

39
Australia Square,
1967, Sydney,
by Harry Seidler.
Australia's first
skyscraper with
a circular tube
structure

accordance with the more common pattern in the West, were changing the face of central city areas around the Pacific Rim. Just as in the West, few of these single buildings merit a second glance, though many grab for attention. However, a small but growing number of buildings of the highest calibre were built – and continue to be built – across the region.

After Palmer & Turner's Hongkong and Shanghai Bank, the next tall buildings of note in the region were built not in East Asia but in Australia. Constructed to meet the needs of Australia's ongoing evolution from a manufacturing economy to a service economy, Australia Square (39) of 1967 in Sydney, by Harry Seidler with Pier Luigi Nervi, was the country's first genuine skyscraper and only the second tall building after Goldberg's Marina City to have a circular-tube structure of reinforced

concrete (40). With its tapering, fin-shaped columns on the perimeter wall and deep, double-skinned inner core, the structure provides great lateral rigidity and column-free spaces in between. Taking a leaf from the Rockefeller Center, the architect also provided ample public space around the base for Sydneysiders' recreation. When it was built, Australia Square was the tallest structure then in the southern hemisphere, but it was easily topped less than a decade later by the 228-metre-high MLC Centre (41) of 1975, also in Sydney and by the same design team. Ultra-slim in proportion, the off-white, eight-sided, reinforced-concrete tower with its tapering corner columns and sculpted edge beams doubling as sunshades – one of the first office buildings in the country to be designed for the local climate – remains one of the city's great landmarks.

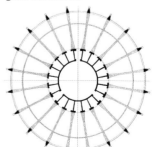

40
Australia Square, 1967, Sydney, by Harry Seidler, left ample open space for public use

41
MLC Centre,
1975, Sydney,
by Harry Seidler.
The slim structure
was made possible
by large perimeter
tapered columns

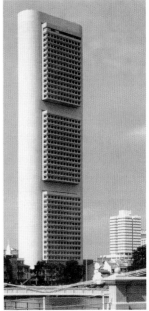

42
Overseas
Chinese Banking
Corporation
Centre, 1976,
Singapore, by
I. M. Pei. Stacks
of floors are
supported by
massive transfer
beams spanning
between service
cores

44
Hongkong and
Shanghai Bank,
1986, Hong Kong,
by Foster and
Partners. The steel
megastructure
is broken down
into stacks of
suspended floors,
creating vertical
'villages'

43
Hongkong and
Shanghai Bank,
1986, Hong Kong,
by Foster and
Partners. The
eight-storey-high
banking hall and
glazed 'underbellly'
through which
customers pass
to and from the
street below

The diminutive island state of Singapore, where land is as scarce as it is in Hong Kong, was next to reach for the sky. As with most tall buildings in the region during this period, clients frequently turned to foreign architects for expertise and experience. The Overseas Chinese Banking Corporation (OCBC) Centre (42) of 1976, by I. M. Pei with engineers Arup, created its own genre with a unique reinforced-concrete structure composed of three stacks of columned floors, each supported by a pair of massive transfer beams connecting to semicircular service towers each side. The resultant column-free spaces above and below the transfer beams allow for conference rooms and a great banking hall on the ground floor. Singapore's highest building upon completion, the OCBC was also overtaken in just a few years by the Overseas Union Bank (OUB) Centre completed in 1986 by Kenzo Tange Associates. Built in the same

45
Standard Bank,
1970,
Johannesburg,
by Hentrich-
Petschnigg &
Partners, one of
the first towers to
have suspended
floors

area close to the Singapore River, the triangular geometry of the tower gives the building a slim outline, belying its great size.

Confident spirit

It was the third headquarters for the Hongkong and Shanghai Bank (44), however, with its all-steel megastructure, suspended floors and Japanese aesthetic, that most captured the confident spirit of the region. Also completed in 1986 and built on the same site as its predecessor by Foster and Partners with Arup, the bank incorporated numerous innovations in office planning, structural design and computerised fabrication methods – the latter being the first such use on a large scale in the construction industry.

Before the Hongkong Bank, the only office tower to be built with suspended floors was the steel-and-concrete Standard Bank (45) of 1970 in Johannesburg, by Hentrich-Petschnigg & Partners – the designers of the Thyssenhaus – where all the floors were suspended in stacks from intermediate branch-like beams cantilevered from a central core. By contrast, the Hongkong Bank's giant trusses transfer the load of each stack of floors to stout four-legged supports on each side of the building. The arrangement creates fully glazed, column-free floors at all levels, interrupted only by thin hanging struts midway, and permitting cross-views right through either side of the building. The main trusses are incorporated into double-height intermediate floors, breaking down the tall building into identifiable zones or 'villages' and providing large spaces for canteens, refuge areas – fireproof safe havens – and lift lobbies. A completely open pedestrian route underneath the building allows passers-by to gaze up through its glazed underbelly into the eight-storey-high banking hall above (43). The constricted site necessitated the prefabrication

47
Century Tower,
1991, Tokyo,
by Foster and
Partners. The
earthquake-proof
steel structure
recalls traditional
Japanese forms

46
Lippo Centre,
1988, Hong
Kong, by Paul
Rudolph. The
faceted-glass
mirror walls
reflect the
surrounding city

of the entire superstructure, with different parts being shipped in from three continents.

Also in central Hong Kong, the twin towers of the Lippo Centre (46) of 1988, by Paul Rudolph, have conventional core structures enlivened by faceted glass walls. Multilevel open public terraces beneath the towers provide welcome shaded spaces. Situated close to the Hongkong Bank, the Bank of China (36, 48) of 1989, by I. M. Pei with engineers Robertson and Fowler, was for a few years the tallest building in Hong Kong and a conscious symbol of China's forthcoming takeover and domination of the colony. The first building to compete in height with the Peak, the Bank of China has a clearly

expressed triangulated steel structure that stops off in angled segments at different heights like the Sears Tower. Internally, however, the structure more closely resembles the John Hancock Center's, with large corner columns taking the loads from diagonal members.

In Japan, despite the earlier promise shown by the Metabolists, as well as huge government investment in building and infrastructure programmes to help stimulate the country's flagging economy, little vertical architecture of distinction has yet been produced, most designers' energy seemingly going into other kinds of project. The modestly scaled and very Japanese-looking Century Tower (47) of 1991

48
Bank of China,
1989, Hong Kong,
by I. M. Pei, a
symbol of the end
of colonial rule

50
Grande Arche,
1989, Paris, by
Johan Otto von
Spreckelsen.
The monumental
structure was
inspired by the
Arc de Triomphe

49
Umeda Sky
Building, 1993,
Osaka, by
Hiroshi Hara, a
prototypical 'city
in the sky'

51
Petronas Towers,
1997, Kuala
Lumpur, by Cesar
Pelli. The twin
towers are joined
by a two-storey-
high steel bridge

52
Following pages:
Shanghai World
Financial Centre,
to be completed
2006, Shanghai,
by Kohn Pederson
Fox. This will be
the world's tallest
building – until
Hong Kong's
Kowloon MTR
Tower is built

in Tokyo, by Foster and Partners with Arup, and the bridged twin towers of the Umeda Sky Building (49) of 1993 in Osaka, by Hiroshi Hara with engineer Toshihiko Kimura, are two notable exceptions. The former has many of the same features as the Hongkong Bank but has a unique, earthquake-proof structure of its own and a rich mixture of uses, including a sports club and below-ground art gallery. The latter owes something both to the Metabolists and to the Grande Arche (50) of 1989 in Paris, by Johan Otto von Spreckelsen. However, where the monumental Grande Arche has a relatively pure form in the Modernist tradition, the Umeda Building is purposely designed as a miniature 'city in the sky' with criss-crossing bridges and escalators and numerous other extensions, giving it the image and inclusive hustle and bustle of a real city.

Taking the crown

Unexpectedly, it was not Tokyo but the Malaysian capital, Kuala Lumpur, that finally took the crown from the Sears Tower. At the time of writing, the 452-metre-high Petronas Towers (2, 51), completed in 1997 by Cesar Pelli with engineers Thornton-Tomasetti and Ranhill Bersekutu, remain the tallest buildings in the world. But, for all their record-breaking size – the combined volume of the towers is around 3,000,000 cubic metres – and plan forms based on Islamic geometrical patterns (not local but borrowed from the Middle East), the twin towers, with their stepped and pointed profiles and glittering stainless-steel claddings, are in many ways a nostalgic throwback to the first golden age of skyscrapers in North America. The towers are also the tallest reinforced-concrete structures in the world, this more familiar material being chosen over steel, despite the extra weight involved, as the preferred local form of construction. The conventional structure is stiffened by floor girders tying the perimeter columns to the core to form an integrated whole. Two smaller cylinders looking like booster rockets to the rear of each tower provide additional space at the lower levels. A steel two-storey bridge supported by two pairs of struts midway connects the towers at the same height as the rear cylinders, suggesting a symbolic gateway to the city.

The gleaming twin towers and their tenuous link are now as much a part of people's image of Kuala Lumpur as the Chrysler Building that inspired them is part of the image of New York. Ironically, like the Chrysler, the Petronas Towers were completed just when the country was struck by a major international financial crisis. Happily, despite the many disparaging and even gleeful comments in the West at the time about 'stillborn' and prestige projects, both the city and the country weathered the storm better than most, justifying the builders' faith in their enterprise.

The heir-in-waiting, the 492-metre Shanghai World Financial Centre (52), to be completed in 2006 by Kohn Pederson Fox (KPF) with engineers Shimizu Corporation, is shaped – or rather 'sculpted', as the architects describe it – like an enormous chisel. Progressively narrowing on two curved faces from a square base to finish in a narrow line at the top, the steel-framed structure has a flattened top portion pierced by an enormous circular hole to reduce wind pressures at this point. The combination of a square plan and a round hole in the top was suggested by the ancient Chinese conception of the earth as a square and the sky as a circle. Whether it will be perceived in this way or not – prominent buildings have a notorious tendency to acquire unintended interpretations, by no means all negative – the sculptural power of the design is beyond question, proclaiming Shanghai's status as a world city of top rank.

53
Previous page:
Swiss Re Tower,
2003, London,
by Foster and
Partners, detail

While the number of tall buildings being built in Asia Pacific is a direct result of larger developments in that region, other global factors, even broader and more important in their impact, are also having their effect on the shape of vertical architecture.

Increasing concerns about the potentially catastrophic effects of global warming on the planetary ecology have overtaken post-war fears of a nuclear holocaust as the primary threat to human survival. No longer able to ignore increasing evidence of the role fossil fuels play in the production of greenhouse gases, international and national institutions are belatedly responding to the growing crisis. Universal as well as local guidelines have been drawn up for restricting the use of fossil fuels and eventually replacing them with alternative and less damaging sources of power, especially renewable sources such as solar energy and wind- or wave-driven turbines. Sustainable development – defined by the Brundtland Commission in 1987 as 'development that meets the needs of the present without compromising the ability of future generations to meet their own needs' – is now accepted, in principle at least, by a growing number of governments as a primary objective to be incorporated into all future planning. Correspondingly, sustainable design has come to mean energy-saving approaches that respect natural ecologies and raise the quality of the environment.

Vernacular models

While the concept of sustainability is becoming accepted by architects and planners as well as by relevant public and private institutions, the continuing lack of worldwide consensus on what specific actions should be taken, and the snail's pace of implementing those that are already agreed, gives little cause for satisfaction or

confidence. Rather than wait for such a consensus to materialise, some national and city governments as well as individual designers are making their own decisions and working towards sustainable goals that often go well beyond current international requirements.

In doing so, many designers have looked to history and to vernacular architecture in particular, searching for models that incorporate sustainable principles of design that could have relevance for today's buildings. For example, since the builders of vernacular architecture in the past had no 'active' or mechanical means of ventilating or cooling their buildings in hot climates, they had by necessity to devise non-mechanical or 'passive' methods of climate control. These included using materials with low conductivity, shading walls from the direct rays of the sun, and planning interiors and openings to encourage the maximum flow of cool air through rooms. For cold climates they used the opposite tactics, preventing heat from escaping and using the mass of the walls to store more heat, whether generated by internal fires or by the occupants themselves. In some parts of the world, particularly the Middle East, devices such as wind scoops and wind towers are used to capture and exploit any external air movement and bring it into the building (54). The grouping of buildings also greatly affects their response to climate. Detached houses are effective in hot, humid climates since they allow cool breezes to penetrate the house from all sides. But in hot, dry climates or cold climates terraced houses or tight clusters are better since each dwelling helps to protect its neighbours, either from direct sun or loss of heat.

However, while such lessons can and have been readily transferred from vernacular houses to modern houses and other small building types such as schools, community buildings and so on, they are less easily transferred to large modern

54
Wind catchers are traditionally used in the Middle East to draw cooling air movement into buildings

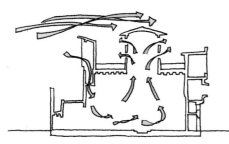

55
Ministry of
Education and
Health, 1942,
Rio de Janeiro, by
Lúcio Costa with
Oscar Niemeyer et
al., the first use of
external sunshades
on a modern tall
building

building types for which there are no historical precedents, either of scale or complexity. Office towers present special problems in this regard, since the large internal spaces they require make it difficult to achieve adequate levels of natural lighting or ventilation in the deeper parts of the structure. Strong winds or driving rain on the higher parts of a building, especially very tall structures, also mitigate against keeping windows open all of the time, further complicating matters.

The invention of mechanical air-conditioning by Willis Carrier in America in 1939 and its widespread use in the post-war years effectively removed such problems, shaping vertical architecture in the latter half of the twentieth century as much as the Otis lift had in the first half – though not without creating other problems. Encouraged by clients eager for larger amounts of rentable space, designers increased the depth of offices, further reducing the penetration of natural light and increasing the need for artificial lighting, hence using more energy. While fully glazed and sealed curtain walls, as pioneered by Mies van der Rohe and Skidmore, Owings, & Merrill, allowed in more light, they only further aggravated the situation, since the increased solar gain had to be offset by the cooling system, hence using more energy again. Health problems, both physical and psychological, arising from the artificial conditions and people's inability to open windows or control the interior environment in any way, have added to the drawbacks. By ignoring the external climate, architects and their clients also ignored important differences in regional conditions, endlessly reproducing the familiar standardised tower forms people have grown to know the world over.

Lessons from the south

The most important early examples of the adaptation of vernacular models of sustainable design to vertical architecture occurred in those parts of the developing world, particularly in the southern hemisphere, where there was a demand for tall buildings but where air-conditioning technology was not yet available or was considered too expensive. The Ministry of Education and Health (55) of 1942 in Rio de Janeiro, by Lúcio Costa and a team including Oscar Niemeyer with Le Corbusier as consultant, was the first tall building to use large exterior sunshades or *brise-soleils* across its entire façade. Although modest in scale, it had a great impact in the post-war years on both large and small buildings throughout the Tropics, suggesting that modern architecture and new building types could be successfully adapted

56
Grosvenor Place,
1988, Sydney,
by Harry Seidler.
Pre-cast concrete
sunshades are
fixed at different
angles according to
the path of the sun

to different regions and climates. The American International Assurance Building of 1964 in Kuala Lumpur, by John Graham with Palmer & Turner, which still stands, is one of many of the same genre and has a dense metal sunscreen that keeps off the heavy tropical rains as well as providing protection from sun and glare.

Despite the temporary fuel shortages caused by the OPEC oil embargo of 1973–74 and the subsequent rise in prices, the eventual near-universal acceptance of air-conditioning as a normal requirement for office buildings cut short such moves towards sustainability. Since maintenance costs do not generally fall within the remit of developers, who are generally interested only in keeping down capital costs, any extra expenses that might be incurred from incorporating sunshades or other measures were invariably rejected, if they were considered at all.

However, beginning in the late 1970s and early 1980s, a small number of designers, backed by bold clients willing to experiment with new ideas or looking for a new image – frequently both – began to reintroduce passive techniques of climate control into office buildings of all kinds and sizes. Usually combined with mechanical systems, they did not eliminate air-conditioning but they reduced maintenance costs while at the same time increasing comfort levels. Further developing his earlier experiments with structural elements that provide limited shading, Harry Seidler, working again with Pier Luigi Nervi on a tower for the Hong Kong Club and Office Building (36) of 1984, included deep, T-shaped, reinforced-concrete beams spanning the full width of the façade. Based on the same team's 40-storey entry for the 1979 Hongkong and Shanghai Bank competition, the heavily sculpted façade with its deep shadows complements the lightweight but similar sunshading techniques used in that bank, which stands opposite.

Taking the same idea a step further, the pre-cast concrete sunshades of Grosvenor Place (56) of 1988 in Sydney, also by Seidler and Nervi, are fixed at different angles around the façade following the path of the sun, providing maximum shading at each point. Also mounted in places where there is no direct sun, they provide effective protection against the glare of the sky, which is extremely strong in Sydney.

Radical turnabout
While such external devices are effective in shading buildings and reducing power costs, they have no significant impact on the internal spaces or configuration of the structure, whether conventional or not. The buildings that employed them could therefore be regarded as variations of other genres of tall building. However, beginning with the National Commercial Bank (57) of 1982 in Jeddah, a quite new genre emerged that broke entirely with previous models of tall buildings.

The bank was designed by Gordon Bunshaft of SOM, the architect of the Lever House, but it could hardly be more different and suggests a radical turnabout by Bunshaft away from the International Style of the earlier building towards a 'regionalised' Modernism in the tradition of Costa's Ministry of Education and Health in Rio. Where Costa found inspiration in the colonial architecture of Brazil – a well-established vernacular in itself – Bunshaft took as his model the courtyard houses of the Arabian Peninsula, creating an inward-looking building with a V-shaped plan (58). The V changes direction twice at different levels up the tower, creating three triangular, recessed 'sky courts' alternating in height on two faces of the building. The only glass walls are placed on the inside faces of the V, where they are shaded from the direct sun, the rest of the building being clad in stone from top to bottom. A vertical flue where the

57
National
Commercial Bank,
1982, Jeddah, by
Skidmore, Owings,
& Merrill. Deeply
recessed sky
courts, inspired
by vernacular
architecture,
shade the glass
walls

58
National
Commercial Bank,
1982, Jeddah, by
Skidmore, Owings,
& Merrill. Plans
showing how the
triangular sky
courts rotate up
the building

60
Kanchanjunga
Apartments, 1983,
New Bombay, by
Charles Correa.
The double-height
sky courts are
based on vernacular
courtyard house
forms

59
Previous pages:
Darmala Building,
1982, Jakarta,
by Paul Rudolph.
The large concrete
shades mimic
traditional
roof forms

alternating triangles overlap creates a 'stack effect', encouraging air movement through the sky courts and upwards out through the top of the building, helping to cool the glass faces. Equally unusually, the service core is situated to one side of the building so that it does not interfere with the internal office spaces and can provide additional shade on that side.

While the interior of the building is entirely air-conditioned – the extreme heat and dusty conditions of the desert region rule out natural ventilation – the design reduces the external temperature at the glass face by as much as 10° Centigrade, resulting in substantial energy savings. In addition to reducing energy costs, the sky courts afford pleasant landscaped spaces where employees can step outside and enjoy some fresh air. The only weakness of the design is the ambiguous scale that the solid mass and

deep recesses convey, which makes the building difficult to read at a distance.

Bunshaft's success in abstracting the lessons of vernacular architecture without succumbing to kitsch imitation, though rare, is replicated in a number of key projects by other architects in different parts of the world, comprising a regionalist school of vertical architecture. The Kanchanjunga Apartments (60) of 1983 in New Bombay, by Charles Correa, are designed on similar principles but on a much smaller scale, and are also based on the vernacular courtyard houses of the region. Designed with maximum surface area because of the subtropical climate, the tower block incorporates double-height sky courts, providing generous, private, open spaces while allowing air to pass through all the rooms, most of which have two exterior walls (61). The Grange Road Condominiums (62)

61
Kanchanjunga
Apartments, 1983,
New Bombay, by
Charles Correa.
A section through
two apartments
showing the
principle of
cross-ventilation

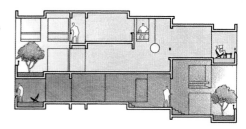

63
Menara Mesiniaga,
1992, Kuala
Lumpur, by T. R.
Hamzah & Yeang,
a small-scale
example of Ken
Yeang's bioclimatic
design approach

62
Grange Road
Condominiums,
1987, Singapore,
by Paul Rudolph.
The large surface
area and shaded
terraces are well
suited to the
Tropics

of 1987 in Singapore, by Paul Rudolph, belong
in the same genre. But instead of the alternating
solids and voids of the Kanchanjunga Apartments,
which reflect local building techniques, Rudolf
adopted an open concrete-framed construction
more in keeping with the framed building tradition
and tropical climate in South-East Asia.

Taking a more literal approach to vernacular
traditions, the concrete-framed Darmala Building
(59, 64) of 1982 in Jakarta, also by Rudolph,
has pitched roofs and large overhangs based
on regional forms. Teetering just on the edge of
direct imitation, the concrete roofs provide shade
and shelter to the windows and open terraces at
each level and help to shed the heavy rainfall.
Completed to a lower height than originally
planned, the office tower has large, open,
semi-private spaces at ground level, similar
to Rudolph's Lippo Centre in Hong Kong.

In the same sky-court genre as the National
Commercial Bank, the Menara Mesiniaga (63)
of 1992, by T. R. Hamzah & Yeang, situated
on the outskirts of Kuala Lumpur, is the most
successful of Ken Yeang's early experiments in
the development of his 'bioclimatic skyscraper'
concept. One of the first architects to apply
ecological principles of design to tall buildings,
Yeang has developed a consistent theoretical
and practical approach to designing energy-
efficient buildings for the Tropics and other parts
of the world. Though too small to be described
as a skyscraper, Menara Mesiniaga embodies
many of the features characteristic of the
architect's more recent and much taller
buildings. Borrowing from local techniques
of climate control but taking a more abstract
approach than Rudolph, Yeang covered the
circular structure with two kinds of sunshade,

66
Commerzbank,
1997, Frankfurt,
by Foster and
Partners. The
double-skinned
climate wall
permits natural
ventilation for 80
per cent of the year

one solid and one permeable, each designed according to its position in relation to the sunpath. As with the National Commercial Bank, the service core is placed to one side but integrated with the plan, where it helps to shield the building and can be naturally ventilated. Spiralling triple-height sky courts cut into the side of the circular open structure to create shaded 'breakout spaces' adjacent to the office floors, encouraging regular use and allowing extra light to reach the centre of the building, which is occupied by glazed conference rooms. (Like the National Commercial Bank, the Menara Mesiniaga is fully air-conditioned but benefits from the sunshades and related features by reduced energy costs.) An exposed-concrete frame with circular columns pokes up above the topmost level, helping to tie the pie-shaped floors together and suggesting that, if so desired, the building might be extended.

New era
All of the tall and not-so-tall buildings described so far in this chapter have one or more distinctive features, whether in their skilful use of natural ventilation and light, their external sunshades, or their plan forms and sky courts, which contribute significantly to the reduction of energy use and the improvement of environmental quality. Accordingly, each in its own way marks a step, small or large, on the long and hard road to sustainability.

The Commerzbank (66), completed in 1997 in Frankfurt by Foster and Partners with Arup, incorporates all of these features (save for the external sunshades, which were not required in that location) as well as many innovations of its own. Together they create the most complete synthesis of sustainable design principles for tall buildings achieved up to that time. Though the plan typology is similar to the National Commercial Bank's, the combined reinforced-concrete and steel structure is totally different, designed to cope with the greater lateral wind forces to which it is subject. Rigidity is provided by pairs of large concrete slab columns in each rounded corner, the three corners being tied together by eight-storey stacks of steel-beamed floors. Each stack acts like a giant truss so that columns and trusses combined form a tube structure much like the great American towers. Service cores are also grouped in the corners, leaving unobstructed floor spaces in between. Where the National Commercial Bank's sky courts are open, the Commerzbank's planted 'sky gardens' are closed by four-storey-high glass walls, sheltering the gardens behind and making them available throughout the year for informal working meetings as well as recreation (65). Each wing is fully glazed on both sides, allowing maximum penetration of natural light as well as views in both directions, either across the gardens or directly outside.

In order to use as much glass for the exterior walls as possible without incurring the usual penalties, the architects, based on their earlier experience in Germany, designed a special 'climate wall' comprising two glass skins, one fixed, one openable. The fixed outside skin has a permanent open slot at the bottom of each window so that when the internal window is opened fresh air is drawn into the interior. If the weather become severe, the windows are automatically closed and the building reverts to its mechanical systems. This hybrid system – the first of its kind to be used in a very tall building – enables the bank to be naturally ventilated for as much as 80 per cent of the year, exceeding the designers' expectations by a full quarter.

Virtual prototypes
The computer-based technologies used in the design and testing of the Commerzbank when it was being developed are as important as the

65
Commerzbank,
1997, Frankfurt,
by Foster and
Partners. The large
sky gardens are
used throughout
the year

68
Swiss Re Tower,
2003, London,
by Foster and
Partners. The
unique structure
was shaped to
minimise
resistance to
wind forces

70
Swiss Re Tower,
2003, London,
by Foster and
Partners. Spiralling
sky courts provide
recreational and
meeting spaces

actual physical structure, and the project
could not have been achieved without them.
Computerised building management systems,
or BMSs, which monitor and control a building's
environmental systems, ensuring the most
efficient use of energy, have been in use since
the 1980s. However, their efficiency can be
assessed only after the system has already
been designed and built into the structure
and the main performance parameters have
been set. For the Commerzbank, the architects
and their environmental engineers, Roger
Preston & Partners, employed state-of-the-art
computer techniques and 'virtual prototypes' to
simulate the likely performance of the building's
design and climate-control systems under all
likely weathers and internal conditions. Testing
of the virtual prototypes was supplemented by
wind-tunnel tests on a model of the structure
and its surroundings, including all buildings
within a 480-metre radius.

Designed by the same team according to
similar ecological principles, the bullet-shaped
structure of the Swiss Re Tower (53, 67, 68),
completed in 2003 in London, is the result of
rigorous testing with virtual prototypes for wind
resistance and other criteria, in which all aspects
of the building's environmental performance
were thoroughly investigated. The circular form,
curved vertically so that it narrows towards the
bottom as well as the top, presents the least
possible resistance to wind forces (69), while
at the same time fitting neatly into the square
in the City of London where it stands. The helical
steel structure – also a unique design – gives the
lightweight building all the strength it needs to
withstand whatever wind forces it encounters.
Parametric modelling, another cutting-edge,
computer technique, was used throughout
the design process, automatically counting
the implications of any changes to one aspect
or system for all other aspects or components.

In addition to an iconic shape and special
structure, the most striking features of the tower
are its spiralling sky courts winding their way up
the full height of the building like a giant stairway.
The numerous courts provide sociable spaces
while at the same time acting as the building's
lungs (70). Fresh air drawn in from outside
through slots in the façade at the edges of the
floor plates is passed over the courts before
circulating through the building. As with the
Frankfurt tower, a combined system of natural
and mechanical ventilation reduces energy
consumption dramatically.

With its streamlined shape, internal gardens
and energy efficiency, Swiss Re bears as much
resemblance to early skyscrapers as does a
space rocket to a First World War biplane. The
next steps in the evolution of vertical architecture
are likely to be generated, however, not by any
single design but by changes in urban culture.

69
Swiss Re Tower,
2003, London,
by Foster and
Partners. Computer
simulation of wind
forces on the
streamlined tower

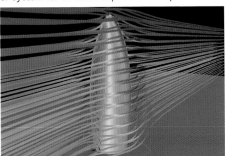

5
CHANGING
URBAN FORM

72
Los Angeles,
1980. The central
business district
viewed from the
suburbs

73
Ebenezer Howard's
Satellite Towns,
1902. Howard's
concept for
controlling the
growth of cities
was dependent
upon efficient
transport links

71
Previous page:
London Bridge
Tower, London,
by Renzo Piano
Building Workshop,
a 'shard of glass'
pointing skywards

As with the buildings themselves, the urban context in which tall buildings have evolved has changed dramatically since their Chicago origins, reflecting both social and technological developments. In particular, the mass production of affordable automobiles spurred a massive population shift from the cities to the suburbs in all parts of the developed world in the second half of the twentieth century, producing the familiar concentric pattern of a high-density city centre surrounded by endless, low-density suburbs (72). So long as it lasted, the availability of cheap fuel, combined with the widespread use of the telephone, made distances between friends or home and workplace seem less important than they used to be.

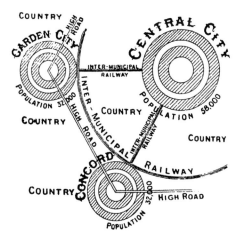

Costs of dispersal

Concerned at the effect of these changes on the countryside, planning authorities in England and Sweden initiated ambitious programmes for 'exporting' the growth of their capitals to surrounding rings of New Towns of 60,000 and more people. Based on Ebenezer Howard's concept of Satellite Towns, part of his Garden City theory (73), the low-density settlements were separated from the capital by 'green belts' – areas of open land where new building was restricted – and were intended to offer new places of employment as well as decent, low-cost housing.

In actuality, the New Towns of London and Stockholm never attracted sufficient businesses or industries to compete with the city, turning instead into 'dormitories' occupied principally by commuters and their families. Often criticised for their dull architecture and lack of physical or social identity, they were also unable to compete with the great diversity of activities available in larger conurbations. Crucially, while the New Towns around Stockholm were connected to the city from the outset by efficient

mass rapid transit (MRT) systems (74), as proposed by Howard in his original plan, London's New Towns lacked the same speedy connections and remained relatively isolated, both from the city and from each other, further reducing their viability.

Instead of being stabilised, as was anticipated, the populations of Greater London and other major cities around the world have continued to grow, creating more suburbs and still more commuters. Despite the dispersal of many industries and businesses, not everyone is able to find both work and a place to live close together in the outer fringes, and most have to travel long distances even if they do not work in the city centre.

As popular as the detached, single-family house with its own garage and garden still is, the costs of urban dispersal are now increasingly seen to outweigh their benefits. Commuters are faced with ever longer, more expensive and more uncomfortable trips between home and work as overstretched and – particularly in the case of London – underfunded transportation systems fail to keep up with the pace of growth. Though

74
Map of Stockholm
showing MRT links
with surrounding
New Towns

often touted as a solution, teleworking – where people work from home via the Internet – also has its limitations, not least the social isolation involved. Even enthusiasts admit it is unlikely to displace normal methods of working for the vast majority of the population, though it may continue to complement them.

If these factors were not enough to persuade doubters, the environmental costs – both local and planetary – of fuelling the relentlessly growing streams of traffic upon which all dispersed cities depend, especially in America and Australia (next to America, Australia has the most suburbanised population and lowest-density cities in the world), have convinced many architects and planners that human society as a whole can no longer continue like this. If we are to survive and to reverse the damage already done, they argue, we must live and build differently.

Densification

75
Capita Centre,
1989, Sydney,
by Harry Seidler.
The interior of the
cramped building
is cut away to
create open sky
gardens and let
in daylight

A contrary trend to urban dispersal has been seen in cities around the world, in which increasing numbers of people, especially young couples and single persons, have chosen an urban lifestyle over the fading attractions of suburbia. Encouraged by government grants to renovate rundown properties and invest in urban homes, combined with public and private redevelopment programmes, they have helped to regenerate city centres. 'Densification' – meaning raising the densities of urban areas through redevelopment programmes, often involving tall buildings of all kinds, whether commercial, residential or mixed-use – is now a key part of official planning policy in many city governments. Combined with new investment in urban infrastructures and public transportation systems, such measures are aimed at reducing reliance on private transport and consequently on fossil fuels.

Improvements in the design of individual structures, not only as they appear above ground but also in the way they connect with the urban sites in which they stand, where they often make their greatest impact, have also played their part in changing perceptions of vertical architecture, encouraging acceptance of densification. The landscaped public plazas of the Riverside Development of 1986 in Brisbane, Grosvenor Place (76) of 1988 in Sydney, and the QV1 Office Tower of 1991 in Perth, all by Harry Seidler with Pier Luigi Nervi, are good exemplars of how tall buildings can contribute to the quality of urban life. In a similar vein, the Capita Centre (75) of 1989 in Sydney, by the same designers, with its open ground-floor gardens and sky gardens above, shows how green spaces can be incorporated into tall buildings even on the most cramped central city sites. The most recent tall building to grace the Sydney skyline, the mixed-use Aurora Place (77) of 2001, by Renzo Piano

76
Grosvenor Place,
1988, Sydney,
by Harry Seidler.
The covered plaza
below the tower is
a popular meeting
and eating place

78
Millennium Tower
project, 1989,
Tokyo, by Foster
and Partners, a
prototype for the
vertical cities of
the future

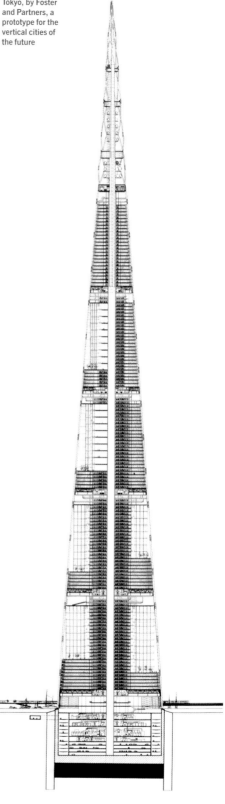

77
Previous page:
Aurora Place,
2001, Sydney,
by Renzo Piano
Building Workshop.
The tower, with its
curved glass façade
and white fretwork,
opens up the
immediate area
at ground level

Building Workshop, makes a virtue of its corner site, creating an open public space between its two towers, each of which is designed quite differently according to its orientation. In addition to enhancing their sites, all these buildings incorporate energy-saving features and, in the case of Aurora Place, naturally ventilated 'winter gardens'.

While tall buildings are invariably associated with central city sites and large groups of similar structures, new patterns of urban development are emerging in which isolated examples, or 'stand-alone' tall buildings play an important role, either as landmarks or as self-contained urban nodes in themselves. The idea of a self-contained, stand-alone tall building is taken to an extreme with Foster and Partners' 840-metre-high Millennium Tower concept (78, 79) designed in 1989 for Tokyo Bay. Aiming to help solve the problem of Tokyo's growing population and land shortage, the architects drew the same conclusion as had Kenzo Tange in the 1960s and took to the waters of Tokyo Bay. However, instead of expanding horizontally and filling most of the Bay, as Tange's project did, Foster and Partners' tower grows skywards, limiting the amount of water covered. The multi-use tower has a cone-shaped, helical, outer steel frame and an inner circular core of reinforced-concrete columns – a tube-within-a-tube – tied together at intermediate levels by deep horizontal steel trusses, giving it immense strength and the ability to withstand both wind forces and earthquakes. The high spaces below each truss serve as refuge centres as well as 'district' centres, breaking down the enormous height of the tower into distinct neighbourhood zones. A vertical 'metro system', based on the electromagnetic technology developed for high-speed railways and able to move both horizontally and vertically, was designed to take passengers rapidly around the building.

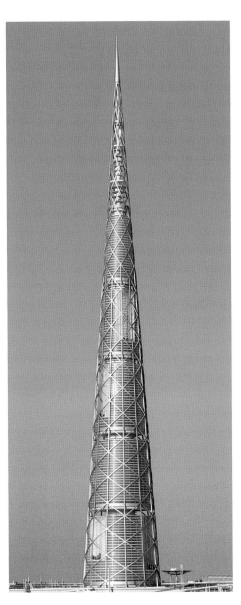

79
Millennium Tower
project, 1989,
Tokyo, by Foster
and Partners. The
tower is structured
vertically into
distinct zones
or districts like
a small city

Dispersed high-rise

Another genre of stand-alone tower varies
in size from a modest but relatively impressive
(when compared with its low-rise surroundings)
20 storeys to over 70 storeys. Belonging to
neither concentrated high-rise, high-density
city centres, nor dispersed low-rise, low-density
city fringes, these buildings suggest an entirely
new category of 'dispersed high-rise' urban form
(81). Making small footprints relative to their
size, such towers, if carefully sited, can provide
much-needed modern accommodation within
older parts of cities with minimal disturbance
to the existing urban fabric, revitalising the
area. Sited in between cities or on their fringes,
single towers can have similarly beneficial
effects, taking up minimal ground space and
leaving continuous green spaces – 'ecological
corridors' – through which plants and wildlife
can spread freely.

   At the lower end of the range, the Menara
Umno (83) of 1998 in Georgetown, Penang,
by T. R. Hamzah & Yeang, stands on Jalan
MacAlister, a broad, straight avenue running
through an area of low-rise 'shop–houses' – a
common, mixed-use Asian building type – at
a considerable distance from the historical
centre of the former colonial town. Designed in
response to the tropical climate in accordance
with Yeang's bioclimatic principles, the building
has a number of original features, including the
use of fins or 'wing walls' at both ends of its slim
concrete structure to channel fresh air through
the tower, which is partly naturally ventilated.

   Standing on its own artificial island in the
Arabian Gulf several hundred metres offshore
and several kilometres from the city centre, the
321-metre-high Burj Al Arab Hotel (82) of 1999
in Dubai, by W. S. Atkins, with its concrete-
framed structure and tensioned fabric covering,
makes an extraordinary landmark along the dead-
flat coastline, looking like a great billowing sail.

81
Kuala Lumpur
seen from the top
of Telekom Tower.
The pattern of
dispersed high rise
is clearly visible

80
Telekom Tower,
2001, Kuala
Lumpur, by Hijjas
Kasturi Associates.
The tower is
situated well
outside the city,
close to the
MRT line

82
Burj Al Arab Hotel,
1999, Dubai, by
W. S. Atkins. The
321-metre-high
hotel stands on
its own artificial
island in the Gulf

83
Menara Umno,
1998, Georgetown,
by T. R. Hamzah &
Yeang. The slim
tower makes a
distinctive but
sympathetic
contrast to the
surrounding
vernacular
buildings

84
Al Faisaliah Tower,
2000, Riyadh,
by Foster and
Partners. The
exotic-looking,
energy-efficient
tower is part of a
large mixed-use
complex

85
Wienerberg Twin
Towers, 2001,
Vienna, by
Massimiliano
Fuksas.
The bridged,
transparent
towers anticipate
the trend towards
linking tall
buildings

In the same region, the Al Faisaliah Tower (84), completed in 2000 in Riyadh by Foster and Partners, with its blue glass sphere framed in the top of a pointed structure, also invokes exotic images of the Arabian Peninsula, though in a more abstract way. Part of a large, mixed-use development in Riyadh's fast-growing commercial district, it was the first skyscraper completed in the city. Covered in aluminium sunshades, the concrete-framed structure is one of the city's few buildings of any kind designed to reduce energy costs and it incorporates numerous related features.

At 310 metres, the Telekom Tower (80) of 2001 near Kuala Lumpur, by Hijjas Kasturi, is in many ways a model of dispersed high-rise building – a common pattern in Asian Pacific countries – as well as a distinguished example of the sky-court genre. Situated over 10 kilometres outside the capital but within walking distance of an MRT station linking it directly to the city, the

Telekom Tower is not only a large structure in itself but also the centrepiece of a landscaped complex including various supporting facilities for the thousands of staff working in the building. It comprises two adjacent curved blocks of column-free office space joined by a service core, with landscaped sky courts on steel platforms suspended between the blocks, flanking the core. The end walls of both reinforced-concrete blocks curve towards the centre, so that the large gardens reduce in size with the height of the building, twisting in a spiralling motion as they do so to form a graceful profile like the folded leaves of a young plant. The organic image is continued in numerous energy-saving features, making this one of the most advanced buildings of its kind in the region.

European Renaissance
Europe is now surprising the world with its own renaissance in vertical architecture. Continental Europeans have always enjoyed a stronger urban culture than North Americans or Australians or even the English – Scottish cities, with their tradition of apartment buildings, are in many ways more like Continental cities than English ones – all of whom have strong suburban cultures. However, like the English, they have long shared an instinctive distrust of tall buildings. That too is also now changing as awareness of the need for densification spreads and innovations in vertical architecture are publicised.

The new openness towards tall buildings was heralded by the remarkable Tour Sans Fin, or Endless Tower, of 1989, by Jean Nouvel with Arup, an unbuilt project for a 420-metre-high office tower in Paris. Situated in the Défense district, next to the Grande Arche, the tower has a diameter of one-tenth its height – the slimmest height-to-width ratio of any skyscraper design up to that time. Any excessive swaying – a

88
Montevideo, to be
completed 2005,
Rotterdam, by
Mecanoo. The
tower will be the
tallest apartment
building in the
Netherlands

potentially serious problem with such a slim design, sufficient to cause motion sickness – is counteracted by a 600-tonne swinging weight placed in the top of the tower like a giant pendulum, its motion dampened to reduce the sway by half.

Completed in 2001, the Wienerberg Twin Towers (85) in Vienna, by Massimiliano Fuksas, are distinguished by the many links between the two elegant glass-walled slabs, suggestive of the joined towers of early visionaries. (What the architect could not have known when he designed them was that, following the disaster of 11 September 2001, such links between tall buildings would quickly become regarded as

essential safety features.) The Uptown Munchen (86) of 2003 in Munich, by Ingenhoven Overdiek and Partner, is, at 146 metres high, the first tower to be built in that usually conservative city since the 114-metre Hypobank was finished in 1975. The architects, who helped pioneer the use of double-skinned climate walls for tall buildings, instead chose an economical single glass skin with high thermal- and glare-resistant properties. Natural ventilation is provided through motor-driven circular windows that move outwards like pistons (87).

Numerous other projects for tall buildings now on the drawing board or under construction around the Continent are also exploring diverse approaches to vertical architecture. Designed to be adapted internally to its occupants' needs, at 152 metres high the Montevideo tower (88) in Rotterdam by Mecanoo will be the tallest apartment building in the Netherlands when completed. Parkhaven (89), also in Rotterdam, by Kohn Pederson Fox (KPF), belongs to the tube-structure genre – now obligatory for very tall buildings – and is promoted as a mixed-use vertical city, complete with offices, apartments, hotel, conference facilities, restaurants and so on. At 392 metres high it will eventually be the tallest building on the Continent. Marking a departure from KPF's earlier, more conventional approach to energy use and cladding design, it features a double-skinned climate wall with opening internal windows.

Though much shorter, Hans Hollein's twin PORR Towers (92) in Vienna, with their upper-level bridges and cantilevered elements, will create an easily recognisable landmark, both from outside the city and within the city centre. Also designed for mainly visual effect, the Hotel Nueva Diagonal (93) in Barcelona, by Dominique Perrault, with its vertically shifted slabs and dense envelope of pierced aluminium panels, will come alive mostly at night, when the skin

90
'Turning Torso',
to be completed
2005, Malmö, by
Santiago Calatrava.
The model reveals
the unique concrete
and steel-tensioned
structural design,
inspired by the
human spine
and torso

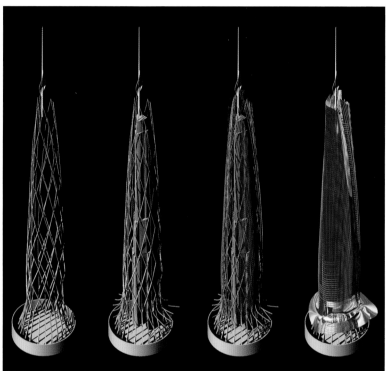

89
Parkhaven,
Rotterdam, by
Kohn Pederson
Fox. The mixed-
use 'vertical city'
has a helical tube
structure similar
to other recent
designs

92
PORR Towers,
Vienna, by Hans
Hollein. The
cantilevered
elements will be
easily recognisable
from a distance

91
Previous page:
Agbar Tower, to
be completed
2004, Barcelona,
by Jean Nouvel.
The bullet-shaped
tower is clad in
coloured glass

with its coloured glass, patterned like a giant stained-glass window, is illuminated. No less colourful than Perrault's design, though not as original as his own Endless Tower, Nouvel's Agbar Tower (91), also in Barcelona, with its bullet-shaped outline and coloured glass skin, confirms the city's long-standing commitment to advanced architecture and urban design.

Sweden has stepped into the fray with the controversial, 200-metre-high 'Turning Torso' (90) in Malmö, by Santiago Calatrava, now under construction. Based on the architect's *Twisting Torso* sculpture, the 52-storey apartment tower comprises nine cubes set at slight angles to each other. Overlooking the Oresund Bridge connecting Sweden with Denmark and the nearby city of Copenhagen, the sculptural form will strike a dramatic pose across the Oresund Strait.

London standing tall

But it is in London that the greatest changes in attitude towards tall buildings are apparent, promising to alter the city's formerly stagnant skyline forever. After the controversial Centre Point, the tallest building to be built in the centre of London for the rest of the twentieth century was the 183-metre-high NatWest Tower 42 of 1980, also by Richard Seifert, situated in the City, the historical and financial heart of London.

It was eventually overtaken in height in 1991 with the completion of One Canada Square (94), by Cesar Pelli, built in the Docklands area of East London. The centrepiece of the vast Canary Wharf redevelopment, London's largest private construction project since the Second World War, the 237-metre-high tower signalled the entrance to the 'Thames Gateway', the planned eastward expansion of London along the Thames. The

93
Hotel Nueva
Diagonal, to be
completed 2005,
Barcelona, by
Dominique
Perrault. The
unstable-looking
massing is
designed to
catch the eye

94
One Canada
Square, 1991,
London, by Cesar
Pelli, the
American-style
centrepiece of
the Canary Wharf
development

city's first American-style skyscraper, Canada Square, despite its considerable distance from the city centre, aroused even more controversy than had Centre Point in its own time and was typically condemned as an American import.

The contrast between the negative reactions little more than a decade ago towards Canada Square and the views expressed by English Heritage and the Council for Architecture and the Built Environment in their report 'Guidance on Tall Buildings' of 2003 could hardly be greater: 'The trend of recent and emerging policy, based on sustainability and demographic considerations, has been to support increased density.' While the report cautions that 'tall buildings are only one possible model for high-density development', the positive results of numerous recent planning applications for tall buildings in London provide clear evidence of

a genuine change of heart and a more open acceptance of vertical architecture of all kinds.

As in Continental Europe and elsewhere, most of these applications are for individual buildings. Many are carefully designed to reduce energy consumption and raise the quality of working and residential conditions. Familiar, though still far from common, features include breakdowns into distinct sections or 'villages'; sky courts or gardens; offset cores and flexible internal spaces; double-skinned climate walls and hybrid systems of natural and mechanical ventilation for offices; and passive systems of heating and cooling for apartments. While the progressive thinking behind the office developments, such as the Heron Tower (96) by KPF, is not unusual now, the proposals for residential towers of almost equal height are far from ordinary. Marks Barfield, the designers of the 200-metre-

95
The Skyhouse
project, London,
by Marks Barfield,
incorporates low-
cost apartments for
key city workers,
as well as energy-
saving features

96
Heron Tower,
London, by Kohn
Pederson Fox, one
of the new genre
of energy-saving
office towers being
built in the City

high Skyhouse (95) project, argue that only by building higher can London provide the additional homes it needs and still retain an acceptable proportion of green open space: 65 per cent of a 1-hectare plot in the case of the Skyhouse. Like Broadway Malyan, the architects of the Sun Tower in Basingstoke, outside London, Marks Barfield propose that a large proportion of the apartments (a third for the former and a quarter for the latter project) be allocated for key workers in the city such as nurses and teachers, to be subsidised by the increased value of the site created by building to a higher density.

Urban nodes
The most far-reaching of the proposed London high-rise projects concern the redevelopment and densification of areas focused around major transportation nodes. Aside from the arguments about 'alien' building types, one of the main criticisms made of Canada Square was that the infrastructure, which included a new but inadequate light rail system, was insufficient to support such a high-density development. The problem was eventually solved by the long-delayed completion of London Underground's Jubilee Line Extension and Canary Wharf Station, but not before the whole development had to be refinanced to overcome lack of investor confidence and tenants.

By contrast the schemes for the Elephant and Castle, Grand Union Paddington Basin and London Bridge areas are all based on existing transportation interchanges. The Elephant and Castle interchange, for example, which lies in the district of Southwark, includes connections with two Underground lines, 23 bus services and an

97
Grand Union
Building, London,
by Richard Rogers
Partnership. The
mixed-use complex
is part of the largest
regeneration
project in the city

99
Elephant and Castle
Garden Towers,
London, by T. R.
Hamzah & Yeang,
bioclimatic
skyscrapers for
the English climate

98
Elephant and
Castle Masterplan,
2000, London,
by Foster and
Partners. Tall
buildings will
be concentrated
around the
transport
interchange

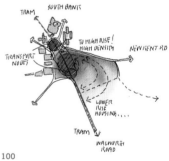

100
Elephant and Castle
Masterplan, 2000,
London, by Foster
and Partners

overland rail service used by commuters from the south. The masterplan drawn up by Foster and Partners (98, 100) proposes an ambitious redevelopment programme aimed at realising the area's full potential, creating a new and vital centre for Southwark and reinforcing the area's role as one of the capital's most important urban nodes. A key part of the strategy is the general densification of the area, involving the construction of several tall buildings providing residential as well as office accommodation, together with a variety of other mixed uses. The logic behind the scheme, as with the other major programmes at Paddington and London Bridge, is to encourage Londoners, whether residents or commuters, to forgo their fuel-guzzling cars in favour of the public transportation systems feeding into the area. There they will find all or most of their needs met within easy walking distance, or they can travel swiftly to another part of the city.

The proposed new buildings include three 'eco-towers' of different heights, designed by T. R. Hamzah & Yeang and appropriately called the Garden Towers (99). The tallest of these, a 35-storey apartment building, has many of the bioclimatic features made familiar by Ken Yeang's work in other, warmer parts of the world, adapted for the English climate. The tower comprises two wings set at a slight angle and linked to each other and to a central core across an open atrium by suspended walkways. The walkways lead onto shared sky gardens at the sides of the towers, overlooking the city. A system of mechanical louvres at each end of the atrium enables the space to be closed or opened according to weather conditions, ventilating the rear of the apartments through the stack effect in the summer and retaining heat in the winter.

Richard Rogers Partnership's Grand Union Building (97) is the focal point of Paddington Basin, an area of regeneration close to the Paddington interchange – the largest programme of its kind in central London. Situated in the attractive canal basin, the mixed-use complex comprises a large office block and three adjacent smaller apartment blocks fronting onto the canal. The large mass of the office building is broken down into six smaller towers of different heights, three on the canal front and three behind, separated by atria, with each tower stepping up to the next, terminating at 217 metres.

Further east, the London Bridge Tower (71, 101), by Renzo Piano Building Workshop with Arup, is the most recent and daring proposal yet to bring new life to London south of the Thames. The second tallest building, after Parkhaven, currently being planned in Europe, at 303 metres high (310 including the spire) the tower will dominate the London skyline – a point of contention hotly debated by many Londoners still hesitant about the future shape of their city. However, the impact will be greatly muted by the elegant pointed form of the tower, which is likened to a shard of glass and will complement the older spires of London across the River Thames.

More importantly, perhaps, the tower sits squarely next to the London Underground and overhead rail links at London Bridge Station, one of the major commuter interchanges in the city. Together with the Elephant and Castle scheme, the London Bridge Tower is designed literally to raise the profile of the South Bank, a process that started optimistically many years ago with the building of the National Theatre and other cultural centres nearby but that has remained stubbornly uncompleted until now. With its vast amount of modern, flexible office space, apart–hotels and shops, the multi-use tower will create a major centre of employment in the area, drawing commuters and local workers onto the tower's doorstep by public transport.

101
London Bridge
Tower, London,
by Renzo
Piano Building
Workshop.
Structured like a
vertical city, the
mixed-use tower
will bring new life
and employment
to the South Bank

6
BUILDING FOR MEGACITIES

103
Apartment Towers,
Sha Tin New Town,
1980s, Hong
Kong, by Hong
Kong Housing
Authority. The
lower floors
typically house
diverse activities

102
Previous page:
Kowloon Station
Tower, to be
completed 2008,
Hong Kong, by
Kohn Pederson
Fox, a vertical city
rising over the main
railway linking Hong
Kong with China

While policies of densification and related urban design programmes can do much to alleviate the problems of Western cities, the rates of population growth and urbanisation in the East present problems of an altogether different scale. Between 1970 and 1990 the number of cities worldwide with a population of over five million grew from 8 to 31, of which 21 are situated in Asia. The largest of these, Greater Tokyo, already has a population of 27 million. Many more Asian cities are predicted to grow to the same size, while over half of Asia's total population will be urbanised within the next twenty years – more than double the figure of 23 per cent in 1970.

The population densities of these giant cities vary greatly from over 95,000 per square kilometre for Hong Kong (106) to just under 10,000 per square kilometre for the Tokyo–Yokohama megalopolis (1991 figures). However, they all exceed Western cities, most by a huge margin, with only Paris, at nearly 8,000 per square kilometre, coming close to Tokyo's density (Table 1). Differences in cultural attitudes also make it sometimes hard for Westerners to appreciate the apparent enthusiasm for high densities and high-rise living in the East, where tall buildings are widely valued as symbols of cultural and social ascendancy. Whereas most tall buildings in the West are offices, invariably concentrated in central business districts (CBDs), the vast majority of tall structures in the larger cities of Asia Pacific are also residential, covering all levels of the economic and social spectrum. Such factors present challenges of a nature and scale beyond conventional Western experience, but from which much may be learnt.

Infrastructure-led development

After its earlier housing programmes, Hong Kong has led the way in creating a model, if a very

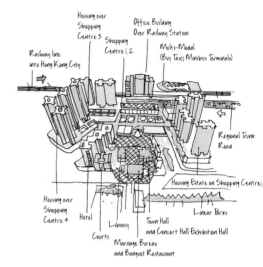

Table 1

Comparative population densities for major Asian and Western cities

	Population (thousands)	Area (km²)	Population (per km²)
Asia Pacific region			
Hong Kong	5,693	60	95,560
Jakarta	9,882	197	50,203
Ho Chi Minh City	3,725	80	46,397
Shanghai	6,936	202	34,334
Bangkok	5,955	264	22,540
Manila	10,156	487	20,859
Seoul	16,792	886	18,958
Taipei	6,695	357	18,732
Beijing	5,762	391	14,732
Singapore	2,719	202	13,458
Osaka–Kobe–Kyoto	13,872	1,282	10,820
Tokyo–Yokohama	27,245	2,821	9,660
Europe and North America			
Paris	8,720	1,119	7,793
New York	14,625	3,300	4,432
Berlin	3,021	710	4,257
London	9,115	2,264	4,027
Los Angeles	10,130	2,875	3,524
Chicago	6,529	1,974	3,308
Houston	2,329	803	2,900

extreme one, for how to deal with high-density large cities both present and future. In 1972 Hong Kong planners embarked on building nine New Towns situated in the New Territories. Modelled, like the parallel programme of New Towns in Singapore, on UK practice, each town was to have its own identity and community facilities, as well as local manufacturing centres for employment, usually built in flatted factories to save space. Together, the towns formed an interlinked system of new settlements providing housing for nearly two million people – half the population growth of Hong Kong during the programme's first decade.

While in principle Hong Kong's New Towns were planned along UK lines, in practice they bore little resemblance to the low-density towns built around London after the war. Ultra-high-density housing clusters such as those in Sha Tin New Town typically take the form of slim towers between 30 and 40 storeys high. Cruciform-shaped to provide maximum wall surface and cross-ventilation in the subtropical climate, the closely packed towers present a daunting spectacle to Western eyes accustomed to low-density cities and lifestyles. However, as with the multifunctional, dense blocks of Kowloon and Hong Kong Island, closer examination of the 'residential' towers and their uses reveals a rich mixture of functions, each situated at a level best suited to its purpose, forming a multilayered vertical community full of vitality (103).

106
The harbour front
in Hong Kong,
the highest-density
city in the world

107
Hong Kong: 'Mark
I' walk-up housing
blocks in the
foreground with
later housing types
in the background

Some recent housing developments, such as Verbena Heights (104) of 1997 in Tseung-Kwan-O New Town in the New Territories and the impressive 45-storey-high Tung Chung Crescent (105) of 1999 in Tung Chung New Town, Hong Kong, both designed by Anthony Ng, combine many of these features together with others reflecting current thinking on sustainable design and energy efficiency. Part of an even larger-scale development, the linked and curved towers of Tung Chung Crescent embrace a pedestrianised community centre, offering all the amenities of a small town in close proximity.

The secret of the success of Hong Kong's New Town strategy compared with London's lies most of all, however, in its extensive mass transit railway (MTR) system linking the towns with the city and with each other, creating an affordable and highly efficient system of public transportation. Linking up with a similarly efficient modern bus service, Hong Kong's public transportation system makes private modes of transport practically unnecessary, resulting in one of the lowest rates of car ownership – relative to its high per capita income – in the world; 44 cars per thousand.

Hong Kong's experience in infrastructure-led development and high-rise, high-density housing is invaluable (107). Nevertheless, as the figures show, the stratospheric population density of the former colony is unique – nearly twice that of Jakarta, the closest example in Asia, it is four times higher than that of most other major cities in the region – and is the product of its special geographical situation and history. While the case for extreme densities and building heights on Hong Kong Island, where additional land for building has had to be artificially created around the harbour, is beyond dispute, some analysts question the need for similarly high densities in the more spacious New Territories. Suggesting that other factors such as land speculation are

the main motivations for Hong Kong's extreme forms of development, they argue for a wider range of densities and housing designs, though still within a strategy of compact, decentralised towns. (The very high price of land on the mainland is the result of government land-control policies designed to raise revenue to compensate for Hong Kong's famously low tax base.)

Constellation cities

The balance struck between building high and maintaining open space on the one hand, and

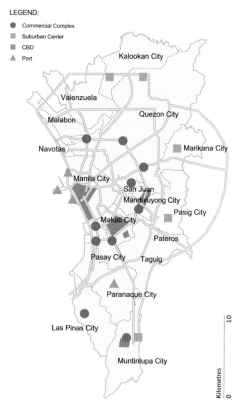

LEGEND:
● Commercial Complex
■ Suburban Center
■ CBD
▲ Port

108
Metro Manila:
The vast
metropolitan area
includes clusters
of smaller cities
and subcentres

building lower but losing open space on the other, may therefore differ greatly from city to city according to history, culture and geography. Manila, with a population density of around 21,000 per square kilometre, is in many ways the opposite of Hong Kong and is typical of many Asian megacities (108). A sprawling conurbation covering over 500 square kilometres with a population of over ten million people, many of whom still endure the same poor conditions once suffered by Hong Kongers, it has grown without any overriding masterplan or coherent system of planning controls. More a collection of poorly linked cities than a single urban entity but with precious little open space left in between any of them, Metro Manila, as the greater area is known, includes eleven large urban centres, such as the City of Manila – the former Spanish colonial port city, and Makati City, the main commercial centres. Like islands situated in a sea of high-density, low-rise structures, including endless squatter settlements as well as villas for the more prosperous, the tall buildings in the affluent high-rise centres presently stand out against the skyline as symbols of inequality as well as modernity. Like many such cities, Manila is beset by horrendous traffic problems but the opening in 2000 of a new MRT system is a hopeful sign of changes to come and will eventually link up all the main centres and the areas in between. Recent high-rise housing projects in outlying districts, though still mostly the preserve of the affluent, also indicate a growing awareness of the need for densification.

Although, with a current population of just over three million, Singapore (109) hardly counts as a megacity, the development of its planning strategy offers a more general model, similar

111
Constellation
city concept,
Singapore, by Liu
Thai Ker. Future
megacities may
be planned as
constellations
of smaller cities
separated by
green belts and
connected by high-
speed rail links

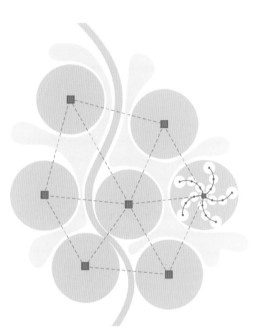

in many ways to Hong Kong's but applicable to a wider range of situations, including those like Manila's involving many subcentres. As in Hong Kong, planners in Singapore in the 1960s initiated an infrastructure-led programme of expansion and decentralisation involving the creation of 23 high-rise, high-density New Towns distributed around the island's MRT system like strings of beads (110). As also in Hong Kong but unlike Metro Manila and almost all other Asian cities, the growth of these towns followed the infrastructure and lines of development laid out in the masterplan, which carefully preserves the maximum amount of open space in between settlements. From 1970 the size of Singapore's larger New Towns grew from a modest, European-style population of 50,000 to between 200,000 and 350,000, creating a hierarchy of 'regional cities' and smaller towns, all interconnected by the island city state's modern public transportation systems to each other and the main city.

As again in Hong Kong, the nature and form of Singapore's high-rise housing has changed along the way, from relatively low, regularly spaced blocks to current projects for 50-storey-high developments that exceed even the most daring projects in Hong Kong (112). Most apartment blocks are likewise enlivened by busy shops and cheap eating places taking up the whole of the ground floor. Increasingly, the tallest buildings have been mixed in with high-density, low-rise housing, creating a still richer mixture. Equally important, Singaporean estates, like their counterparts in Hong Kong, benefit from highly efficient managements who have both the technological know-how and organisational skills to maintain the buildings, and especially their lift systems, in good running order – a crucial factor in the success of high-rise housing that is often overlooked.

Building on Singapore's experience, Liu Thai Ker, the city's former chief planner, has proposed a similar strategy of clustered cities, collectively called a 'constellation city' (111), for dealing with the problems of Asia's megacities. Citing such precedents as the Hague–Rotterdam– Amsterdam cluster totalling four million people, Liu proposes that new large cities be planned and designed at the outset as clusters of independent but interlinked cities of 1.5 to 2.5 million people, each with its own commercial and cultural centres. Separated by green belts in the manner of Ebenezer Howard's Garden City concept, the constellation city idea resembles Howard's in some ways – most especially in the importance given to rapid transportation links. However, constellation cities differ totally from Howard's satellites in their far greater scale, in their more even size and distribution, and in their

110
Concept plan,
1991, Singapore,
by Singapore Urban
Redevelopment
Authority, a
masterplan for the
future growth of
Singapore's New
Towns, showing
a constellation of
regional centres
distributed around
the MRT system

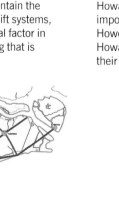

113
New National Board Library Building, to be completed 2004, Singapore, by T. R. Hamzah & Yeang. As densities increase, more building types like this library will be reaching skywards

112
Duxton Plain Public Housing project, 2002, Singapore, by ARC Studio Architecture + Urbanism. 'Sky parks' link the seven 48-storey blocks together in a continuous bent line

higher densities, which Liu considers essential for the preservation of open space. Combining the best of both worlds, the constellation city concept potentially offers the more human scale and sense of identity of a small city with the unlimited range of activities and opportunities of a megacity, available within relatively easy reach from any point in the cluster.

A study carried out at the University of the Philippines in 1999, 'Manila Constellation City 2020', showed that, theoretically at least, existing megacities like Metro Manila, which are already partially but ineffectively structured as constellation cities, could be much improved if treated in a similar way by further intensifying development in the city centres, upgrading transportation links and preserving and enlarging open spaces in between. The difficult process of enlarging open spaces such as those along the

edges of waterways, which are often occupied by squatters, would require rebuilding and densification in those areas to accommodate the same number of people with minimal change in their location and hence their lives. Once a component city has reached a given size and density, the whole network would be extended to grow another new city of approximately the same size but possibly with a different character and orientation towards commerce or culture.

Varied shapes
In accordance with the logic behind London's current major projects, the largest buildings in constellation cities would be concentrated over the main transportation centres, reducing travel times or the need for private transport and making it easier to live in one city and work in another. Some current megatowers in Asia

114
Kowloon Station
Tower, to be
completed 2008,
Hong Kong, by
Kohn Pederson Fox

present models of just this kind. Since the
international airport moved to Chek Lap Kok,
the lack of any height restrictions has produced
a new spate of megatowers in that city: for
example, the 480-metre-high Kowloon Station
Tower (102, 114), by Kohn Pederson Fox,
and the 574-metre-high Kowloon MTR Tower
(116), by Skidmore, Owings, & Merrill, destined
eventually to take the crown from Shanghai.
Both towers are in Hong Kong and both are
located over major transport interchanges.
Designed as parts of a massive land-reclamation
project on the harbour, both are also mixed-use
towers in the vertical-city genre, creating giant
urban hubs and visual focal points for the whole
conurbation. The unusual glass skin of the former
tower, with its shingle-like layered windows and
curved 'skirts' at the bottom, albeit somewhat
contrived, adds to the character of the building.

Other bold schemes in the pipeline suggest
the outlines of the megacities and constellation
cities of the future and the varied shapes of their
taller components. Some projects, like the 100-
metre-high New National Library Board Building
(113) in Singapore, by T. R. Hamzah & Yeang,
involve building types not normally associated
at all with vertical architecture (the National
Library in Paris by Dominique Perrault is another
exception). Based on a similar plan typology
to the architects' Elephant and Castle towers,
the library's overall cubic form – rare in itself
for such a tall building – consists of two smaller
blocks under the same canopy roof, separated
by a naturally lit internal street and connected by
bridges at upper levels. The larger block contains
the library's collections and sits over a naturally
ventilated civic plaza, reinforcing the public
nature of the building – 'a place for people', as
the designers describe it. By the same architects,
the mixed-use Beijing World Science and Trade
Centre comprises a dense group of apartment,
hotel and office towers, each composed of thick

115
Central Chinese
Television Building,
Beijing, by Rem
Koolhaas. The
unique cantilevered
structure involves
revolutionary
engineering
techniques

116
Kowloon MTR
Tower, Hong Kong,
by Skidmore,
Owings, & Merrill.
At 574 metres high
this will be the
tallest building in
the world, but for
how long?

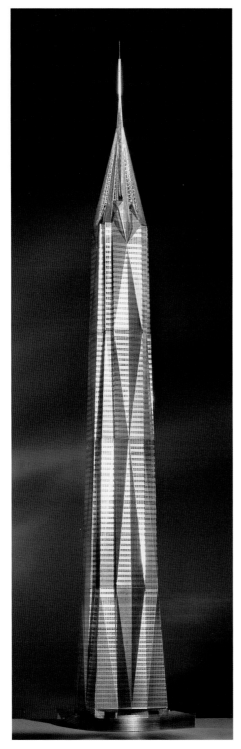

or thin twin slabs according to their function. Designed as a 'self-contained microcosm of the larger city', the complex has its own internal rapid transport system (IRTS) to move people around, connected with the city's primary transport systems.

The Beijing World Centre shows how very high densities might be achieved with the provision of ample open space but without the regimented lines of towers associated with many of Hong Kong's projects and not necessarily at a higher cost. But even Ken Yeang's fluid forms look conservative compared with the extraordinary Central Chinese Television Building (115), part of a large, mixed-use television centre in Beijing by Rem Koolhaas with Arup. Likened to a Chinese puzzle, the unstable-looking steel-framed structure is the joint creation of Koolhaas and Arup's engineer, Cecil Balmond, who has been behind many recent equally unconventional designs for other building types. The apparently random pattern of exposed cross-braces on the façade is a direct expression of the asymmetrical forces at play in the dramatically cantilevered structure. Designed to house the headquarters of CCTV, the building is clearly meant to send a signal to the world that China means to set the pace in vertical architecture, as in other fields.

Japan's Takenaka Company – one of the country's 'Big Five' construction companies – is also rising to the challenge with two projects for vertical cities: the Sky City 1000 (119) and the Holonic Tower (117). As much as 1,000 metres high, the former tower would pierce the clouds, housing 36,000 residents and 100,000 workers in the same structure. Like the earlier Millennium Tower, Sky City and the smaller Holonic Tower raise the possibility of creating whole clusters of similar giants linked up to form larger cities in themselves, leaving minimal footprints on the land and allowing flora and fauna to range freely in between as though in a natural forest.

119
Sky City 1000
project, by
Takenaka Company.
An experimental
design, this 1,000-
metre-high vertical
city would house
36,000 residents
and 100,000
workers

117
Holonic Tower
project, by
Takenaka
Company. This
vertical city would
comprise a linked
cluster of mixed-
use towers

118
Ventiform project,
2001, by Foster
and Partners, one
of a new genre of
streamlined, self-
powered towers

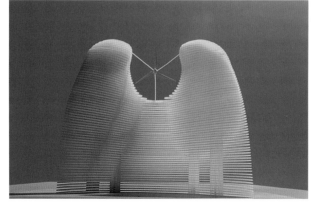

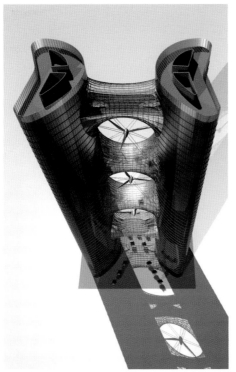

120
Twin Wind Tower
project, 2000,
by University of
Stuttgart School of
Architecture. Wind
turbines housed in
streamlined towers
can generate more
power than free-
standing wind
turbines

Although not as great in scale as some of the above towers, projects like Foster and Partners' Ventiform (118) that incorporate large, relatively silent wind turbines into their structure may eventually have a far greater impact on the future of vertical architecture. Small wind turbines were also incorporated into Richard Rogers Partnership's unbuilt Turbine Tower project for Tokyo of 1996 as well as in Marks Barfield's current Skyhouse project. However, aside from limited streamlining, in neither of these cases could the use of the turbines be said to affect radically the design of the structure.

By contrast, the Ventiform project represents a completely new genre of vertical architecture and sustainable design. As the name implies, the design takes its form from the need to channel wind forces smoothly through the opening in the structure where the wind turbine is fixed. Based on an EU-funded research programme involving private as well as university-based organisations, the design capitalises on the programme's finding that, if surrounding surfaces and housing are designed efficiently, wind turbines set within buildings actually generate more power than free-standing turbines.

As part of the same research programme, a group of architecture students at Stuttgart University, led by Professor Stefan Behling, has produced a series of experimental designs for tall buildings with built-in wind turbines, using the extra wind power gained by height. The designs include floating towers that exploit the high winds across open water, and linked towers with several wind turbines placed in between (120). Like the streamlined Ventiform, these designs are anything but the arbitrary form-making exercises currently in fashion, and have all the sleek purpose of racing cars.

There is in all these experimental projects a positive exchange of ideas between individual building designs and settlement patterns in which new approaches to building cities on a giant scale are constantly emerging. However, if there is one lesson to be learnt from the broad range of projects shown here it is that the days of formulaic solutions in which one concept or schema sets a pattern to be applied everywhere are over. Common and consistent themes there are – but we are more likely to see fragments of many of these ideas appearing together in one form or the other, mixed and blended according to need. The location for such experiments is likely to be just as varied, in both East and West, northern and southern hemispheres, including America, now finally returning to the cutting edge in vertical architecture.

7
AMERICAN
POSTSCRIPT

121
Previous page:
World Trade
Center project,
2002, New York,
by Studio Daniel
Libeskind. The
scheme comprises
several separate
towers of different
heights encircling
the former site of
the twin towers

122
Los Angeles
Courthouse,
Los Angeles, by
Perkins and Will,
one of the first of a
new generation of
towers in America
designed from
sustainable
principles

124
New York Times
Building, to be
completed 2006,
New York, by
Renzo Piano
Building Workshop.
Sunshades made
from white ceramic
cylinders help to
keep energy
costs low

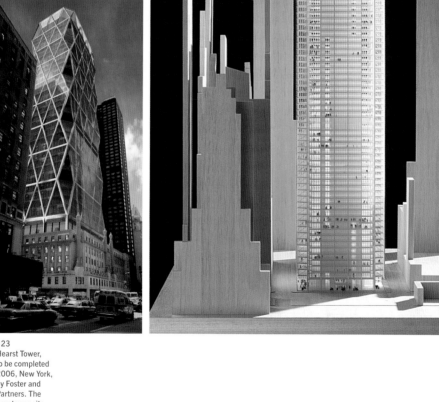

123
Hearst Tower,
to be completed
2006, New York,
by Foster and
Partners. The
new tower sits
inside the shell of
a 1928 building,
which will house
a covered
public plaza

While American architects have been prominent in skyscraper developments abroad, at home they have generally stuck to well tried and trodden pathways, mostly concentrating on the external features of tall buildings and repeating past models. The lack of official support for or professional interest in sustainable design in America relative to other countries has also notably dampened innovation in this area.

However, beginning with the competition for the New York Times Building in New York, the past few years have witnessed a renewed interest in America in innovative vertical architecture. The catastrophic events of 11 September 2001 also focused public and professional attention on skyscrapers in a way no other event could possibly have done. Having lost the lead to others, the country that started it all is finally waking up to the new era and making its own mark – again.

Though relatively small in comparison with other designs of the same genre, the Los Angeles Courthouse (122), by Perkins and Will with Battle McCarthy engineers, is one of the country's first tall buildings to be shaped head to toe by sustainable design principles and is a significant sign of new thinking. Special features include courtrooms naturally lit from two sides, a solar-powered generator on the south wall and below-ground storage systems that provide free cooling for most of the year.

As the heart of the world's first certified megalopolis, stretching all the way from Boston to Washington, it is fitting that New York City should host the search for a new generation of skyscrapers fit for the megacities of tomorrow. The New York Times building competition, won by Renzo Piano Building Workshop in 2000, marked a major turning point, focusing interest once again on creative design in vertical architecture and drawing in fresh talent from abroad. With its delicate, layered skin of white

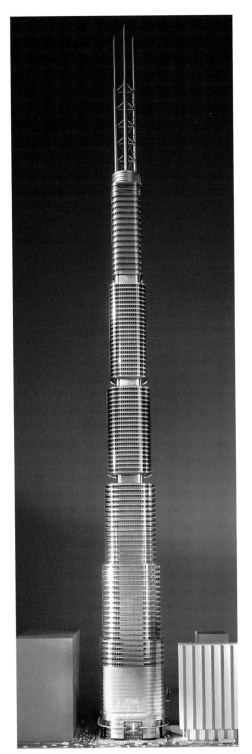

125
7 South Dearborn, Chicago, by Skidmore, Owings, & Merrill. The slim, mixed-use tower has a unique 'stayed-mast' structure

126
World Trade Center
project, 2002,
New York, by
United Architects.
A broad public
'skyway' including
green parks and
other amenities
links the five
towers together

127
World Trade Center
project, 2002,
New York, by
United Architects,
a 'family' of giants

ceramic sunshades over clear glass walls, the building (124) brings a fresh quality of lightness and transparency to the city's skyline as well as a high degree of energy efficiency.

The commission for a new tower for the Hearst Corporation (123) presented Foster and Partners with the difficult problem of integrating the base into the shell of a six-storey building completed by Joseph Urban in 1928. Originally intended to incorporate a tower above, the old building shell will enclose the lower supports of the new tower, creating a large internal toplit plaza with restaurants and exhibition spaces. Using a triangulated steel structure of great strength, the tower is designed in the tradition of the second golden age of American skyscrapers, when engineering and architectural design went hand in hand, to mutual benefit.

The same could be said of SOM's 468-metre-high tower, 7 South Dearborn (125) in Chicago, designed with engineer William Baker. The mixed-use tower derives its ultra-slim profile from a radically new structural genre called the 'stayed-mast' system. Based around a large reinforced-concrete tubular core or 'mast' stiffened by internal cross-walls, a ring of sparsely placed columns provides lateral strength in the lower, wider office floors – the 'stayed' part of the mast – bolstered by 'outrigger trusses' at intermediate levels. The smaller upper apartment floors are cantilevered out from the core, providing column-free, flexible, customised spaces and unobstructed views of the city below.

Following 11 September, safety issues in tall buildings, formerly taken for granted, jumped suddenly to the fore, for a time at least pushing all other considerations aside. New guidelines swiftly drawn up by multidisciplinary research groups included the use of newly developed integrated fireproofing materials capable of protecting steel structures in temperatures of over 2,000° Centigrade (the temperature of burning aviation fuel) for several hours. Other measures suggested were multiple escape routes, including protected lift cores and more stairways, together with 'redundant' structures capable of standing up even after large chunks of a building have been damaged.

Bridged towers – formerly the province of Futurists – of which the Petronas Towers, the Umeda Sky Building and Tung Chung Crescent are still rare built examples, also started to look less like fantasies than practical solutions to the problem of escape, allowing people to cross from one tower to another. The dream of 'cities in the sky' in which the horizontal dimension is treated as importantly as the vertical dimension is now fast becoming reality.

Soon after the disaster, the architectural competition for the redevelopment of the World Trade Center site in Manhattan, now known universally as Ground Zero, presented some of the world's leading architects with the greatest challenge of their careers. Torn between conflicting needs to provide a suitable memorial to the victims of 11 September and to realise the huge value of the cleared site, as well as having

128
World Trade
Center project,
2002, New York, by
Peterson Littenberg,
modestly scaled
with retro styling

129
World Trade
Center project,
2002, New York,
by Richard Meier
and Partners
et al., a monolithic
structure of
identical linked
towers

to integrate their schemes with major transport links below ground, the seven competing teams responded with wildly varying approaches. Some designs were overscaled and, in comparison with the former twin towers, sat awkwardly on the Manhattan skyline. One of the more successful schemes in this respect, the winning design by Studio Daniel Libeskind (121, 134), comprises a cluster of separate, sharply angled towers of different size and height, grouped in a protective arc around the site, the tallest finishing in a distinctive but unobtrusive spire. By far the most modest in scale of all the entries, the relatively conventional design by the New York firm of Peterson Littenberg (128), suffers from its retro styling, making it look almost timid in comparison with other schemes – doubtless eminently buildable but an uninspiring sequel to the former towers.

Significantly, most of the schemes include linked towers, creating the multiple escape routes and horizontal spaces indicative of the new genre. One of these, by Richard Meier and Partners with other American firms (129), comprises two arrays of evenly spaced rectangular towers at right angles to each other. Both sets of towers are bridged at the same regular points, forming a monolithic, gridded structure that overshadows its neighbors. Similarly, the scheme by SOM et al. (131) consists of a giant forest of towers designed with a more irregular geometry but all finishing at the same height, forming a vast, skyscraper-city-within-the-city, each tower capped with a green plaza open to the sky.

130
World Trade
Center project,
2002, New York,
by Foster and
Partners. The
triangulated
structure
represents
a striking new
landmark

131
World Trade Center
project, 2002,
New York, by
Skidmore, Owings,
& Merrill. Each
tower is capped
by a landscaped
'plaza'

132
World Trade
Center project,
2002, New York,
by THINK, an
ephemeral design
comprised of twin
'empty' steel
frames

133
World Trade
Center project,
2002, New York,
by THINK. The
covered plaza at
the base of the
towers

134
World Trade
Center project,
2002, New York,
by Studio Daniel
Libeskind. The
cluster of towers
fits well into the
Manhattan skyline

134
World Trade
Center project,
2002, New York,
by Studio Daniel
Libeskind. The
cluster of towers
fits well into the
Manhattan skyline

By contrast, the twin, triangulated towers by Foster and Partners (130) are designed in the lighter tradition of structural engineering for which the firm is renowned, and seem barely to touch each other. Based on studies on new safety measures for tall buildings produced by the firm with other consultants shortly after 11 September, the design also incorporates state-of-the-art energy-saving features. Even lighter, almost ephemeral in spirit, the two linked towers by THINK (132, 133) are designed as open steel-framed megastructures, containing several enclosed 'buildings' at different heights, but otherwise left completely empty. Intended to be illuminated at night, the towers would form two columns of light reminiscent of the twin vertical searchlights created earlier on the site.

One of the most radical entries, the design by United Architects (126, 127), features a broad public concourse or 'skyway' linking all five towers together in one continuous, sky-high urban space complete with green parks. For all its great size, the eccentrically balanced cluster of towers of differing heights suggests not so much skyscrapers as most people know them but a family of giants gathered for a group photograph, leaning up against each other in casual familiarity. The latest in a long history of efforts to humanise tall buildings – some successful, some less so – the anthropomorphic grouping is symbolic of the great changes in vertical architecture that are now underway, the eventual products of which we can only begin to visualise.

BIBLIOGRAPHY

Abel, Chris, 'Manila Constellation City 2020', unpublished report by theUniversity of the Philippines, Metro Manila, 1999

Abel, Chris, *Architecture and Identity: Responses to Cultural and Technological Change*, Oxford, 2000

Abel, Chris, 'Electronic Ecologies', in *Norman Foster: Works 4*, David Jenkins (ed.), Munich, 2003

Banham, Peter Reyner, *Megastructure: Urban Futures of the Recent Past*, London, 1976

Battle, Guy, and Chris McCarthy, *Wind Towers*, Chichester, 1999

Battle, Guy, and Chris McCarthy, *Sustainable Ecosystems and the Built Environment*, Chichester, 2001

Battle, Guy, and Chris McCarthy, 'Sustainable Towers: Sustainability Brief', Department of Trade and Industry, London, 2002

Burdett, Ricky, Kathryn Firth, Tony Travers and Victoria Scalongne, 'Tall Buildings: Vision of the Future or Victims of the Past?', London School of Economics Cities Programme with Development Securities PLC,London, 2002

Campbell, N. S., and S. Stankovic (eds), 'Wind Energy for the Built Environment: Project WEB', BDSP Partnership with Imperial College, Mecal Applied Mechanics and the University of Stuttgart, London, 2001

Campi, Mario, *Skyscrapers: An Architectural Type of Modern Urbanism*, Basel, Boston and Berlin, 2000

Cervero, Robert, *The Transit Metropolis: A Global Enquiry*, Washington, D.C., and Covelo, 1998

Chung, Judy Chuihua, Jeffrey Inaba, Rem Koolhaas and Sze Tsung Leong (eds), *Great Leap Forward*, Cambridge, Mass., and Cologne, 2001

Condit, Carl W., *The Chicago School of Architecture*, Chicago and London, 1964

Cuthbert, Alexander R. (ed.), *Designing Cities: Critical Readings in Urban Design*, Malden and Oxford, 2003

'Density II', *Architecture and Technology* (Autumn 2002)

Diamond, D., and J. B. McLoughlin (eds), *Architecture, Society and Space: The High-Density Question Re-examined*, Oxford, 1985

Duany, Andres, Elizabeth Plater-Zyberk and Jeff Speck, *Suburban Nation: The Rise of Sprawl and the Decline of the American Dream*, New York, 2000

Echenique, Marcial, and Andrew Saint (eds), *Cities for the New Millennium*, London and New York, 2001

Edwards, Brian, and Paul Hyett, *Rough Guide to Sustainability*, London, 2002

English Heritage and the Commission for Architecture and the Built Environment,'Guidance on Tall Buildings', London, 2003

Fishman, Robert, *Urban Utopias in the Twentieth Century: Ebenezer Howard, Frank Lloyd Wright, Le Corbusier*, Cambridge, Mass., and London, 1982

Fletcher, Banister, *A History of Architecture*, Dan Cruickshank (ed.), Oxford, 1996

Foster and Partners, 'Tall Buildings Study: Safety Considerations After 11 September', London, 2002

Garreta, Ariadna Alvarez (ed.), *Skyscrapers*, Mexico, 2002

Gissen, David (ed.), *Big and Green: Toward Sustainable Architecture in the 21st Century*, exh. cat., National Building Museum, Washington, D.C., 2002

Greater London Authority, 'Interim Strategic Planning Guidance on Tall Buildings, Strategic Views and the Skyline in London', London, 2001

Greater London Authority, 'Towards the London Plan: Initial Proposals for the Mayor's Spatial Development Strategy', London, 2001

Gutierrez, Laurent, Ezio Manzini and Valerie Portefaix (eds), *HK LAB*, Hong Kong, 2002

Huxtable, Ada Louise, *The Tall Building Artistically Considered*, New York, 1984

'Instant China: Notes on an Urban Transformation', *2G International Architectural Review*, 10 (1999)

Jenks, Mike, Elizabeth Burton and Katie Williams (eds), *The Compact City: A Sustainable Urban Form?*, London and New York, 1996

Jenks, Mike, and Rod Burgess (eds), *Compact Cities: Sustainable Urban Forms for Developing Countries*, London and New York, 2000

Ker, Liu Thai, 'The 6th Megacities Lecture: Optimizing Resources', paper presented at the Annual Lecture of the Dutch Megacities Foundation, The Hague, Netherlands, 28 November 2002

Ker, Liu Thai, 'From Megacity to Constellation City: Towards Sustainable Asian Cities', paper presented at the Conference on India, Southeast Asia and the United States: New Opportunities for Understanding and Cooperation, Singapore, 30 January–1 February 1997

Koolhaas, Rem, *Delirious New York: A Retroactive Manifesto for Manhattan*, New York, 1994

Koster, Egbert, and Theo van Oeffelt (eds), *High-Rise in the Netherlands 1990–2000*, Rotterdam, 1997

Maas, Winy, Jacob van Rijs and Richard Koek (eds), *FAR MAX: Excursions on Density*, Rotterdam, 1998

Marsden, Brian S., 'A Pressured Place: the Structural Context of Environmental Planning in Hong Kong', *Planning and Development*, 11 (1995), pp. 9–21

Marshall, J. G., et al. (eds), *Rising High in Harmony*, Hong Kong, 1993

Miao, Pu (ed.), *Public Places in Asia Pacific Cities: Current Issues and Strategies*, Dordrecht, Boston and London, 2001

Nash, Eric P., *Manhattan Skyscrapers*, New York, 1999

Newman, Peter, and Jeffrey Kenworthy, *Sustainability and Cities: Overcoming Automobile Dependence*, Washington, D.C., and Covelo, 1999

Pank, Will, Herbert Girardet and Greg Cox, 'Tall Buildings and Sustainability', The Corporation of London, London, 2002

Shepherd, Roger (ed.), *Skyscraper: The Search for an American Style 1891–1941*, New York, 2003

Sidener, Jack, 'Creating the Exuberant City: Lessons for Seattle from Hong Kong', *Arcade*, 15 (Summer 1997), pp. 32–35

Singapore Urban Redevelopment Authority, 'Living the Next Lap: Towards a Tropical City of Excellence', Singapore, 1991

Soja, Edward W., *Postmetropolis: Critical Studies of Cities and Regions*, Oxford, Melbourne, Berlin, 2000

Sorkin, Michael, and Sharon Zukin (eds), *After the World Trade Center: Rethinking New York City*, New York and London, 2002

Toy, Maggie (ed.), *Reaching for the Skies*, Architectural Design Profile No. 116, 1995.

Wong, A. K., and S. H. K. Yeh (eds), *Housing a Nation: Twenty-Five Years of Public Housing in Singapore*, Singapore, 1985

Yeang, Ken, *The Skyscraper Bioclimatically Considered: A Design Primer*, London, 1997

Yeang, Ken, *Redefining the Skyscraper: A Vertical Theory of Urban Design*, London, 2002

Zaknic, Ivan, Matthew Smith and Dolores Rice (eds), '100 of the World's Tallest Buildings', Council on Tall Buildings and Urban Habitat, Mulgrave, 1998

Zukowsky, John, and Martha Thorne (eds), *Skyscrapers: The New Millennium*, Munich, 2000

PICTURE CREDITS